AFRICAN-AMERICAN FREEDOM SEEKERS

Harford County Maryland

1774–1864

Henry C. Peden, Jr., M.A.

HERITAGE BOOKS
2026

HERITAGE BOOKS

AN IMPRINT OF HERITAGE BOOKS, INC.

Books, CDs, and more—Worldwide

For our listing of thousands of titles see our website
at
www.HeritageBooks.com

Published 2026 by
HERITAGE BOOKS, INC.
Publishing Division
5810 Ruatan Street
Berwyn Heights, MD 20740

International Standard Book Number
Paperbound: 978-0-7884-5415-8

Table of Contents

occurred in Pennsylvania and were connected to Harford County freedom seekers. They are also briefly discussed.

There is some information about accomplices, black and white, who helped in the flight to freedom in Harford County prior to 1864 and also some runaway indentured servants between 1864 and 1882. Even though slavery had ended in Maryland in 1864, some servants thereafter also sought freedom from their unwanted servitude. Finally, any comments by the author are noted in [brackets] herein.

Acknowledgments

Special thanks to James E. Chrismer, retired history teacher and a local expert on African-Americans and the Civil War, for his research and generous contribution of material for this book, especially runaway advertisements in the *Pennsylvania Gazette* and *Pennsylvania Packet*, and relevant copies of information from William Still's book and journals, which made this book more comprehensive.

Thanks go to the Maryland State Archives staff and volunteers who created their on-line "Legacy of Slavery in Maryland" database. This was indeed a tremendous source of information about Harford County runaways.

References have been cited within the text after each entry which also mentions researchers and authors Carolyn G. Adams, Iris L. Barnes, Theodore W. Bean, Constance R. Beims, Jacob Bensen, James E. Chrismer, John A. Comley, Samuel Mason, Jr., William Still, Janet L. Taylor, Christine P. Tolbert, and F. Edward Wright.

Also, thanks to volunteers at the Historical Society of Harford County for maintaining records about African-Americans in their library, archives, and court record files.

Thanks to Jack L. Shagena, Jr., my good friend and colleague, for his guidance, advice and computer expertise.

Introduction

It is estimated that about 100,000 slaves used the Underground Railroad to escape slavery. Many of them came through Maryland via Harford County to cross over the Susquehanna River into Cecil County or follow the river north to Pennsylvania and beyond. The Emancipation Proclamation in 1863 freed many slaves. Maryland slaves were not freed until the Maryland Constitution of 1864.

Harford County was a busy corridor for freedom seekers with stations at the Hays House near Bel Air (now the Hays-Heighe House at Harford Community College), Swallowfield in Berkley (near Darlington) where slaves hid in the ice house, William Worthington's house at Shure's (or Worthington's) Landing near Darlington (house now gone), "Had" Harris House (once located on the Susquehanna River, but now under Conowingo Lake created by the 1928 Conowingo Dam), and Belle Vue Farm near Havre de Grace (on Chesapeake Bay, south of Susquehanna River). Many unidentified homes and buildings secreted African-American freedom seekers along the Susquehanna River.

It is not the purpose of this book to discuss in any detail the Underground Railroad itself; rather, the intent is to identify, as many as possible, those slaves in Harford County who escaped to freedom. Being such a secretive activity made it inherently difficult to find only a few hundred, who are alphabetically arranged within the text by surname. Those without surnames are also arranged alphabetically, like Negro Jack or Mulatto Joe.

There are many advertising notices about runaways from extant Harford County and Pennsylvania newspapers. Such notices gave detailed descriptions. Three nationally significant events – Rope Ferry Incident (1841), Prigg vs. Pennsylvania (1842), and Christiana Resistance (1851) –

About the Author

Henry C. Peden, Jr. is an award-winning author of more than 200 historical and genealogical reference books, and a renowned genealogist and local historian. He is a graduate of Towson University (B. S., M. A.), and a veteran of the Vietnam War (SSgt., USAF). He is a Fellow and Past President of the Historical Society of Harford County and the Maryland Genealogical Society. He is a Past President of the Harford County Genealogical Society, Past President General and co-founder of the Hereditary Order of the Signers of the Bush Declaration (March 22, 1775), and Past President (Laird) of the Highland Society of Harford County. He has partnered with Jack L. Shagena, Jr. to create 25 episodes of a history program titled *Harford's Heritage* for Harford Cable Television. In 2017, the library of the Historical Society of Harford County was named "The Henry C. Peden, Jr. Research Library" in his honor.

Mr. Peden's other books pertaining to African-Americans are *Slaves and Slave Owners, Harford County, Maryland, 1814*, and *African-American Horsemen, Harford County, Maryland,* and *African-American Cemeteries in Harford County, Maryland*, and *African-Americans in Harford County, 1774-1864.*

His historical preservation work has been recognized by the Harford County Government, Harford County Historical Preservation Commission, Maryland General Assembly, The Daughters of the American Revolution, The National Society of U.S. Daughters of 1812, and The Maryland & Pennsylvania Railroad Historical Society. Mr. Peden and wife Veronica reside in Bel Air, MD.

African-American Freedom Seekers Harford County, Maryland 1774-1864

Alkin, William. He was a slave of Sarah Cook and escaped over the Susquehanna River into Pennsylvania with the help of David McCann in 1792. (Ref: Historical Society of Harford County, Court Records Document 30.7.5)

Allen, Amelia. 1860. "State of Maryland, Harford County, to wit: The Jurors of the State of Maryland for the body of Harford County do on their oaths present that Caroline Snoden, late of Harford County aforesaid, free negress, on the Fifteenth day of November in the year of our Lord Eighteen Hundred and Sixty, with force and arms at the County aforesaid, unlawfully did entice, pursude *(sic)* and assist one Amelia Allen, the said Amelia Allen being then and there the slave of one Henry H. Lee, to abscond and run away from her said owner, the said Caroline Snoden, free negress as aforesaid, then and there well knowing the said Amelia Allen to be a slave as aforesaid, contrary to the form of the Act of Assembly in such case made and provided and against the peace, government and dignity of the State. William H. Dallam, State's Attorney for Harford County." (Ref: Historical Society of Harford County, Court Records Document 131.13.5).

Amelia Rebecca Allen (born in February 1847), who was about to abscond, run away and leave Maryland, with others, "she having run away before but was not induced to do so by ill treatment or improper conduct" of her owner Henry H. Lee, was ordered by the court in 1860 to have her service extended until 1 Jan 1875. The court also authorized that she could be sold within or without the limits of the State of Maryland. (Ref: Harford County General Entries Book TSB No. 6, p. 292)

Anderson, George. "Dec 16/54. George Anderson, now Henry Jones, arrived safely [in Philadelphia] from Herberts Cross Roads, where Harman Stump … was a hard man. Geo. is 19 yrs, of age, dark chesnut *(sic)* color, stout made ..." (Ref: William Still's Journal, Philadelphia, 1854)

Archer, Sam. "Sundry Arrivals from Maryland, 1860. Sam Archer was 'to become free at thirty-five years of age.' He had already served thirty years of this time; five years longer seemed age to him. The dangers from other sources presented also a frightful aspect. Sam had seen too many who had stood exactly in the same relations to Slavery and freedom, and not a few were held over their time, or cheated out of their freedom altogether. He stated that his own mother was 'kept over her time,' simply 'that her master might get all her children.' Two boys and two girls were thus gained, and were slaves for life. These facts tended to increase Sam's desire to get away before his time was out; he, therefore, decided to get off via the Underground Railroad. He grew very tired of Bel Air, Harford County, Maryland, and his so-called owner, Thomas Hayes [Hays]. He said that Hayes had used him 'rough,' and he was 'tired of rough treatment.' So, when he got his plans arranged, one morning when he was expected to go forth to an unrequited day's labor, he could not be found. Doubtless, his excited master thought Sam a great thief, to take himself away in the manner that he did, but Sam was not concerned on this point; all that concerned him was as to how he could get to Canada the safest and the quickest. When he reached the Philadelphia station, he felt the day dawned, his joy was full, despite the Fugitive Slave Law." (Ref: *The Underground Railroad*, by William Still, 1871, repr. 1970, pp. 549-550). "Mr. Hays has offered two hundred dollars for the arrest of a negro man named Sam, who ran away one year ago." (Ref: *National American*, 7 Jun 1861)

Baker, William. A slave of Edward Gallop who lived on a farm at Michaelsville, he was married to Harriet Ann Cole (1829-1913), a free Negro woman, daughter of William and Harriet Cole of Havre de Grace, on 25 Oct 1845. Her paternal grandmother was a Bradford who married a Cole and her maternal great-grandmother was a Native American who married an Englishman and they had a daughter who married a man named Lego, native of Guinea who resided on Bush River Neck, and whose daughter Harriet Lego married William Cole and they were parents of Harriet Ann Cole who married William Baker. Harriet subsequently discovered in 1847 that her husband William was about to be sold to Georgia. They escaped with their infant child across the Susquehanna River and settled in Columbia, Lancaster Co., PA. Harriet Baker always believed that she was called to preach and after many arduous labors, including the loss of her home and death of two teenage daughters, she began her ministry in Brownstown, PA. William Baker died in the late 1880s. (Ref: *The Colored Lady Evangelist, Being the Life, Labors and Experiences of Mrs. Harriet A. Baker*, by Rev. John A. Cornley, 1892, pp. 8, 15; Baker information published in *African American National Biography*; Rev. Harriet A. Baker's obituary in *Allentown Democrat*, 3 Mar 1913)

Billingslea, Thomas. "Four Hundred Dollars Reward. – Ran away from the subscriber, on Saturday night, 23rd inst. [1851], Two Boys. Ned Nowland is 5 feet 10 inches high; 20 years old; chesnut *(sic)* color; has a scar on the cheek bone (not recollected which). He wore a black coat and pantaloons; he took a bundle of other clothing with him.

Thomas Billingslea is 5 feet 6 inches high; 21 years old; black; clothing the same as the other. The above reward will be given for both, or $200 for either, if lodged in some jail so I may get them again. Washington M. Slade, Harford County, Maryland, near Abingdon post-office." (Ref: *Baltimore Sun*, 27 Aug 1851)

Bond, Charlotte. "Was committed to the Jail of Baltimore City and County, on the 19th day of July, 1833, by Charles Kernan, Esq., a Justice of the Peace, in and for the City of Baltimore, as a runaway, a mulatto woman who calls herself Charlotte Bond or Stansbury; says she belongs to Mrs. Mary Smithson living in Harford County near Belair. Said mulatto woman is about 35 years of age, 4 feet 9 1-2 inches high, has a scar on her right thumb caused by the cut of an axe, also, one on her left arm by being scratched by a cat. Had on when committed, a blue and yellow calico frock, blue and red handkerchief on her head, black silk handkerchief on her neck, check apron and old pair of shoes. The owner of the above-described mulatto woman is requested to come forward, prove property, pay charges and take her away, otherwise she will be discharged according to law. D. W. Hudson, Warden, Baltimore City and County Jail." (Ref: *Commercial Chronicle and Daily Intelligencer*, 29 Jul 1833)

WAS COMMITTED to the Jail of Baltimore City and County, on the 19th day of July, 1833, by Charles Kernan Esq. a Justice of the Peace, in and for the City of Baltimore, as a runaway, a mulatto woman who calls herself CHARLOTTE BOND, or STANSBURY; says she belongs to Mrs. Mary Smithson living in Harford County near Belair. Said mulatto woman is about 35 years of age, 4 feet 9 1-2 inches high, has a scar on her right thumb caused by the cut of an axe, also, one on her left arm by being scratched by a cat. Had on when committed, a blue and yellow calico frock, blue and red handkerchief on her head, black silk handkerchief on her neck, check apron and old pair of shoes.

The owner of the above described mulatto woman is requested to come forward, prove property, pay charges and take her away, otherwise she will be discharged according to law.

D. W. HUDSON, Warden,

J27 p Baltimore City and, County Jail.

Brown, Dick. "Notice – Was committed on the third day of March, 1822, to the Jail of Baltimore County, as a runaway, a black negro man by the name of Dick Brown, property of Charles Hall, of Harford County. He is about five feet five inches high; had on when committed a blue cloth coat, blue pantaloons, white vest, fine shoes and stockings. The owner of the above-described negro is desired to come forward, prove property, pay charges and take him away, or he will otherwise be discharged according to law. Sheppard C. Leakin, Sh'ff. of Baltimore County." (Ref: *Daily National Intelligencer*, 15 May 1822)

Brown, Jacob. "$40 Reward. Ran Away from the Subscriber on the 15th inst., a Negro Man named Jacob Brown; about five feet ten inches high; one of his middle fingers off at the first joint – about 43 years of age. If taken in this State, twenty dollars, and if taken out of this State and secured so that I get him again, forty dollars will be given by James B. Amos. Harford County, Md., August 29, 1828." (Ref: *Independent Citizen*, 4 Sep 1828)

$40 REWARD.

RAN AWAY from the Subscriber on the 15th inst. a Negro Man named Jacob Brown; about five feet ten inches high; one of his middle fingers off at the first joint—about 43 years of age.

If taken in this State, twenty dollars, and if taken out of this State and secured so that I get him again, forty dollars will be given by

JAMES B. AMOS.

Harford County, Md. August 29, 1828. sep 3 3t

Brown, Jesse. "One Hundred and Fifty Dollars Reward. – Ran away from the subscriber, on Saturday night, the 1st of June [1850], a Negro Man, named Jesse Brown. He took with him four pair of pants – two pair were of white cotton goods – and three summer coats, two hats, and one pair of fine half boots. He is about 21 years old, small size, with a scar on his forehead; stammers very much when spoken to. The above reward will be paid if taken out of the State, $100 if taken within the State, and $50 if taken in the County and returned to me, or secured so that I may get him. Thos. B. Swartz, Abingdon, Harford County, Md. [Elkton (Md.) Whig, and Gazette, York, Pa., copy to amount of $1 each and charge this office.]" (Ref: *Baltimore Sun*, 5 Jun 1850; *The Cecil Whig*, 8 Jun 1850)

Butler, James. "Two Thousand Dollars Reward. – The above reward will be paid for the apprehension of four blacks [Edward Morgan, Henry Johnson, Stephen Butler, Jim Butler], who escaped on Sunday last [31 May 1857]. It is supposed they have made their way to Pennsylvania. $500 will be paid for either, so that we can get them again. Jim Butler is a dark-complexioned negro, 5 feet 8 or 9 nine inches [high]; is rather sullen when spoken to; face rough; aged about 21 years. The clothing not recollected. They had black frock coats and slouch hats with them." (Ref: *Baltimore Sun*, 5 Jun 1857)

"From the Underground Rail Road Records. The following memorandum is made, which, if not too late, may afford some light to 'Elizabeth Brown and Thomas Johnson,' if they have not already gone the way of the 'lost cause.' Jim Butler is a dark-complexioned negro, five feet eight or nine inches, is rather sullen when spoken to; face rough; aged about twenty-one years. The clothing not recollected. They had black frock coats and slouch hats with them. Any information of them, address Elizabeth Brown, Sandy Hook P.O., or of Thomas Johnson, Abingdon P. O., Harford County, Md." A later entry stated, "James is about twenty-one years of age, full black, and medium size. As he had been worked hard on poor fare, he concluded to leave, in company with his brother [Stephen] and two cousins, leaving his parents in slavery; owned by the 'Widow Pyle,' who was also the owner of himself. She was upwards of eighty, very passionate and ill-natured, although a member of the Presbyterian Church. James may be worth $1,400." (Ref: *The Underground Railroad Authentic Narratives and First-Hand Accounts*, by William Still, 1872, repr. 2007, pp. 40-41)

Butler, John Alexander. 1857. "Arrival from Arlington [Darlington], MD [to Philadelphia]. John Alexander Butler, William Henry Hipkins, John Henry Moore and George

Hill. This party made, at first sight, a favorable impression; they represented the bone and sinew of the slave class of Arlington *(sic)*, and upon investigation the Committee felt assured that they would carry with them to Canada industry and determination such as would tell well for the race.

"John Alexander Butler was about twenty-nine years of age, well made, dark color, and intelligent. He assured the Committee that he had been hampered by Slavery from his birth, and that in consequence thereof he had suffered serious hardships. He said that a man by the name of Wm. Ford, belonging to the Methodist Church at Arlington *(sic)*, had defrauded him of his just rights, and had compelled him to work on his farm for nothing; also [her] had deprived him of an education, and had kept him in poverty and ignorance all his life.

"In going over the manner in which he had been treated, he added that not only was his master a hard man, but that his wife and children partook of the same evil spirit; 'they were all hard.' True, they had but three slaves to oppress, but these they spared not.

"John was a married man, and spoke affectionately of his wife and children, who he had to leave behind at Cross-Roads ... When charges or statements were made by fugitives against those from whom they escaped, particular pains were taken to find out if such statements could be verified; if the explanation appeared valid, the facts as given were entered on the books." (Ref: *The Underground Railroad*, by William Still, 1871, repr. 1970, pp. 433-434; *A Journey Through Berkley, Maryland*, by Constance R. Beims and Christine P. Tolbert, 2003, pp. 45-46)

Butler, Stephen. "Two Thousand Dollars Reward. – The above reward will be paid for the apprehension of four blacks [Edward Morgan, Henry Johnson, Stephen Butler,

Jim Butler], who escaped on Sunday last [31 May 1857]. It is supposed they have made their way to Pennsylvania. $500 will be paid for either, so that we can get them again. Stephen Butler is a dark-complexioned negro about five feet seven inches [high], has a pleasant countenance, with a scar above his eye; plays on the violin, about 22 years old. The clothing not recollected. They had black frock coats and slouch hats with them. Any information of them, address Elizabeth Brown, Sandy Hook P. O., or of Thomas Johnson, Abingdon P. O., Harford County, Md." (Ref: *Baltimore Sun*, 5 Jun 1857)

"From the Underground Rail Road Records. The following memorandum is made, which, if not too late, may afford some light to 'Elizabeth Brown and Thomas Johnson,' if they have not already gone the way of the 'lost cause.' Stephen is a brother of James and is about the same size, though a year older. His experience differed in no material respect from his brother's; was owned by the same woman [Pyle], whom he 'hated for her bad treatment' of him. Would bring $1,400 perhaps." (Ref: *The Underground Railroad Authentic Narratives and First-Hand Accounts*, by William Still, 1872, repr. 2007, pp. 40-41)

Carlisle, William. "Runaway Slaves. – On Saturday night last [25 Jun 1859] some eight or nine slaves ran away from their owners at Perrymansville and that vicinity. Three of them belonged to A. D. Keen, Esq." (Ref: *Baltimore Sun*, 2 Jul 1859)

"Arrival from Maryland [in Philadelphia]. Jim Kell, Charles Heath, William Carlisle, Charles Ringgold, Thomas Maxwell, and Samuel Smith ... William was of also unmixed blood, shrewd and wide-awake for his years – had been ground down under the heel of Aquila Cain [Aquila D. Keen]. He left his mother and two sisters ... After being furnished with food clothing, and free tickets, they were forwarded on in triumph and full of hope." While he was in bondage, "William had been stripped naked, and frequently and cruelly cowhided." (Ref: *The Underground Railroad*, by William Still, 1871, repr. 1970, pp. 521-522)

Runaway Slaves.—On Saturday night last some eight or nine slaves ran away from their owners at Perrymansville and that vicinity. Three of them belonged to A. D. Keen, Esq.

Chambers, Teney. "Notice. Was committed, on the 27th day of May, 1825, to the jail of Baltimore County, as a runaway, by Joseph B. Elliott, Esq., a Justice of the Peace for the city of Baltimore, a negro girl named Teney Chambers, says she belongs to Abraham Jarrett, of Havre de Grace, Maryland. She is five feet three and a half inches high, about 24 years old, had on when committed, striped Gingham frock, shoes without stockings, two scars by a burn on her neck. The owner of the above negro is desired to come forward, prove property, pay charges, and take her away, or otherwise she will be discharged according to law. S. Barry, Sheriff, Baltimore County." (Ref: *Daily National Intelligencer*, 8 Jun 1825)

Chapman, Mark. "Runaway [1836] committed to Harford County jail, negro man, Mark Chapman, light complexion, about six feet high, scar on forehead above the right eye, middle finger on one of his hands considerably crooked, about 35 years of age, scar on fore finger of his left hand, and one on his left leg appears to be occasioned by a burn, says he is a miller and came from Virginia, Fairfax County. Preston McComas, Sheriff." (Ref: *Harford Republican*, 17 Mar 1836)

Chase, John. "Superior Court. – Before Judge Frick. – The following business occupied yesterday [18 Jan 1855]: John Chase vs. B. M. & N. L. Campbell, a petition for freedom. Chase was taken up in Harford County, as a runaway slave, and kept in jail sixty days. On being asked, while there, for his freedom papers, he gave as a reason for having none that he was from Pennsylvania, whereupon he was sold to Messrs. Campbell, under the act of Assembly prohibiting free negroes from coming into the State. The petitioner now alleges that he never was in Pennsylvania, and introduces testimony to that effect, and his counsel urge that the judgment under which he was sold was illegal. Verdict for petitioner. Bartol and Farnandis for petitioner; Pitts for respondents." (Ref: *Baltimore Sun*, 19 Jan 1855)

Christiana Resistance. "'Freedom Started in Christiana – The Harford County Connection.' September 11, 2001 … We recall where we were and remember what occurred at 8:45 A.M. We are also aware of the lengthy military aftermath of that horrible tragedy. However, very few Americans realize that on the exact day 150 years earlier, at a nearly-precise moment of the morning, a similar historically critical event occurred: The September 11, 1851 confrontation at Christiana, PA, that contributed to the outbreak of the American Civil War, the preservation of the United States, and the consequent freedom of some 4 million African Americans. Of the leaders on the side of freedom at what historians today call the Christiana Resistance, nearly half had Harford County roots.

"Basic reference works describe the Christiana Resistance in straight-forward fashion. In the fall of 1851 Baltimore County plantation owner Edward Gorsuch learned that three enslaved men who had fled his property three years previously had been located living as free persons in Lancaster County, PA. Emboldened by passage of the Federal Fugitive Slave Act of 1850 that empowered slave holders, the incensed Gorsuch gathered a posse of several men that included his son Dickinson. Gorsuch journeyed to Pennsylvania to secure an arrest warrant, engaged a federal marshal, wended his way to the hamlet of Christiana (33 miles from Havre de Grace), and planned to capture his slaves at the home of William Parker where Gorsuch believed his fugitives dwelled. The idea was to intimidate the occupants with force, demand their surrender and return the runaways to Maryland.

"William Parker may have just been a name to Gorsuch but was widely known in the area as a staunch defender of the rights of African Americans. The 29-year-old runaway laborer from Anne Arundel County had lived in the Lancaster area for twelve years, during which he aided fugitives, supported the rights of freed Blacks, and helped the Lancaster Black Self-Protection Society to thwart who regularly came into the area seeking Black victims to send to Maryland for sale.

"Arriving at dawn, Gorsuch's party quickly realized that Parker and the nearby black community had been warned of their coming. Nonetheless the group surrounded the small two-story stone house that sat in a group of trees in an otherwise open field. The home held several freedom seekers, including at least two of Gorsuch's escapees, as well as Parker's 34-year-old wife Eliza, sister-in-law Hannah (perhaps 39), and brother-in-law Alex Pinkney.

"Almost immediately Gorsuch verbally and physically challenged an infuriated Parker at the front door but failed to move him. The Baltimore Countians pulled back and threatened to set the house ablaze. Several random shots rang out as the home's residents retreated to the second floor. Eliza Parker, from the garret, sounded a pre-arranged horn blast that attracted a volley of shots from the posse and a crowd of mostly black neighbors armed with agricultural tools including corn cutters and firearms to defy the invaders.

"A stalemate slightly under two hours settled in as Goruch's men considered their options. Meanwhile Parker and Gorsuch continued to exchange a series of threats, convinced of the righteousness of their causes, and made obvious their unwillingness to back down. Eventually shots rang out from both sides, and a melee involving the principals and the assembled crowd ensued. In the end Gorsuch was killed and his son suffered a near-fatal wound. The remainder of the party retreated.

"Of the persons with Parker at least five had fled Harford County in the 1840s. These included Eliza Ann Elizabeth Howard Parker, her sister Hannah Pinckney, two brothers, and their 51-year-old mother Cassie Harris. Hannah's married name of Pinckney strongly suggests that her husband may also have originated in Harford County.

"Back in Harford County, 42-year-old planter Albert Davis claimed all of these individuals as his property. Davis, whose father Dr. Elijah Davis at one time kept 34 enslaved persons, had inherited Belle Vue, a 300-plus-acre estate abutting Oakington and Swan Harbor on the Chesapeake Bay near Havre de Grace. According to Cassie, her son had escaped on Easter 1843 and her daughters soon followed. She claimed Davis blamed her, demanded she tell him the whereabouts of her children, and threatened to have everyone hung if they did not return. When Cassie proved unable to help, Davis banished the then 43-year-old unskilled house servant from the plantation.

"In the following days Cassie's children had made their way across the Mason-Dixon Line to Lancaster

County. Three years later, in 1846, Eliza married William Parker and had three children. At some point Hannah met and married Pinckney. Cassie herself somehow found her way to the group and helped care for the children.

"Following the violence of September 11, 1851 local, state and federal law enforcement authorities descended on the area as pro-slavers insisted that laws protecting life and property be upheld. Officials rounded up almost anyone involved with the revolt, queried witnesses, and conducted hearings. Eventually, federal officials oddly charged 41 persons, black and white, with treason against the United States, and offense that is extremely difficult to prove. When a friendly Philadelphia jury in late November quickly found innocent an anti-slavery Quaker who prosecutors believed represented their strongest case, authorities dropped all charges. Every defendant, Eliza, Hannah and Cassie included, went free.

"In the immediate aftermath of the resistance, William Parker, Alex Pinckney, and Abraham John, a fugitive from Cecil County, had fled north. Aided by the Pownalls, a neighboring Quaker family active with the Underground Railroad, the threesome headed straight to Rochester, NY and Frederick Douglass. The nationally prominent Douglass, the Maryland-born fugitive whose own escape took him through Harford County, made arrangements to get the Christiana party into Canada beyond the authority of law enforcers from the United States.

"Life for William Parker and his fellow outlaws in a foreign country was difficult. With their dark skin and without any particular skills the men found work scarce and lodging even more so. Parker especially wrote of missing his family. Emily finally arrived in Toronto on November 24, 1851, but had been forced to leave the children behind in the care of her mother. During her trek northward she had been followed by Albert Davis, and kidnappers had once taken her into custody. Hannah, her child, and the three Parker children eventually reunited in Canada.

"In time the families settled in Buxton, a small town in southwest Ontario, barely 50 miles from Detroit [MI]. Founded in 1849 by Presbyterian ministers, the hamlet of about 400 persons in 1852 served as a refuge for African American freedom seekers. For the most part the emigrants disappeared into the past, although William learned to read and write, became a reporter for Douglass' newspaper *The North Star*, took part in local politics, and served with the town government. He returned briefly to Christiana in 1871. One source indicates that William lived out his life in the U.S. and died in Kenton, OH on April 14, 1891. That report cannot be verified.

"As a wife of the 19th century in a rural area, Eliza was characteristically busy. She and William had up to seven additional children while in Canada and operated a 50-acre farm that they shared with another African-American couple. They helped establish and were members of the North Buxton British Methodist Episcopal Church, in whose cemetery Eliza rests following her death in 1899 at age 82. Nearby is a gravestone of a Hannah Peaker (d. 1889, age 77), likely Hannah Pinckney as Harford County African-American residents would surmise. Efforts to identify the Parker and Pinckney children have proven unsuccessful. In 2009 one of Eliza's multi-generational grandchildren helped produce a local PBS film on her life, and four years later another granddaughter erected an impressive brass gravestone marker to describe Eliza's remarkable life.

"The story of Cassie is the most intriguing of all the Davis fugitives. She comes, goes, and disappears in the

Havre de Grace-to-Christiana-to-Buxton saga. At least twice her family left her behind (at Belle Vue and after Christiana). Additionally, after the trial in Philadelphia, Eliza and Hannah headed north to Canada without making any real provision for their mother to follow. Months after the November decision and apparently after enduring the weather, Cassie had enough; she went to the courts and asked she be returned to Maryland. The court honored her request, and presumably Cassie Harris returned to Havre de Grace and Belle Vue Farm for the rest of her life.

"Make no mistake about the national significance of the Christiana Resistance. It and the trial that followed constituted the first real test of the Fugitive Law of 1850, a measure political and economic conservatives regarded as crucial to their defense of property in the form of slaves. Anti-Slavery forces cheered the outcome of the trial that set free scores of the law's opponents and put a lie to the hopes of defenders of states' rights and slavery, who regarded as appalling the overt individual and judicial attacks on their rights.

"Tension between Free and Slave states mounted during the subsequent decade. Events such as Bleeding Kansas, publication of *Uncle Tom's Cabin*, the Dred Scott Decision, the formation of the Republican Party, the Raid on Harper's Ferry, and the election of Abraham Lincoln – all enflamed the respective forces. The war came bringing death and destruction but also the preservation of the Union, the Emancipation Proclamation, and the 13th Amendment. Frederick Douglass himself noted, "The battle for liberty began in Christiana." Red banners on street poles proclaim proudly as visitors enter the 1200-person borough that 'Freedom Began Here.'" (Ref: Article researched by James E. Chrismer, of Bel Air, Harford County, MD, 2019)

Christy, Jack. "Arrival from Belle Air [into Philadelphia in 1858]. Julius Smith, Wife Mary, and Boy James, Henry and Edward Smith, and Jack Christy. While this party was very respectable in regard to numbers and enlisted much sympathy, still they had no wounds or bruises to exhibit, or very hard reports to make relative to their bondage. The treatment that had been meted out to them was about as tolerant as Slavery could well afford; and the physical condition of the passengers bore evidence that they had been used to something better than herring and corn cake for a diet." Nothing was specifically written about Jack Christy. (Ref: *The Underground Railroad*, by William Still, 1871, repr. 1970, pp. 473-474)

Coleman (Colerain?), Jake. He was born on 1 Oct 1837 and was a runaway slave in the early 1850s. He was caught and ordered by the court to serve his owner for 25 years.

The court also authorized that he could be sold within or without the limits of the State of Maryland. (Ref: Harford County General Entries Book TSB No. 6, p. 269)

Cook, Daniel. "Committed as a Runaway. Was committed to the jail of Harford County, Md., on the 5th inst., by John T. Bradberry, a justice of the peace in and for the town of Havre de Grace in said County, a Negro Man who calls himself Daniel Cook, supposed to be a runaway slave. Said negro is about 25 years old, about five feet eight or nine inches high, rather stoutly made, and of dark color. The owner, if any, is hereby notified to come and get him, otherwise he will be disposed of according to law. J. E. Bateman, Sh'ff." (Ref: *The Southern Aegis*, 20 Jul 1861)

Committed as a Runaway.

WAS committed to the jail of Harford County, Md., on the 5th inst., by John T. Bradberry, a justice of the peace in and for the town of Havre de Grace in said county, a NEGRO MAN who calls himself Daniel Cook, supposed to be a runaway slave. Said negro is about 25 years old, about five feet eight or nine inches high, rather stoutly made, and of dark color. The owner, if any, is hereby notified to come and get him, otherwise he will be disposed of according to law.

ju22 J. E. BATEMAN, Sh'ff.

Croken, James. "Notice. Was taken up and lodged in Elkton jail, as a runaway, on the 25th day of August last [1854], a yellow man rather grey, about fifty-five years of age, calls himself James Croken, has on a round satinet jacket, black-silk vest, white cotton pants, black wool hat and boots. He says he is from Harford and is free. He is somewhat deranged in mind. If not claimed, he will be discharged according to law. Robert M. Walmsley, Sheriff." (Ref: *Cecil Democrat*, 9 Sep 1854)

NOTICE.

WAS taken up and lodged in Elkton jail, as a runaway, on the 25th day of August last, a yellow man rather grey, about fifty-five years of age, calls himself James Croken, has on a round satinet jacket, black-silk vest, white cotton pants, black wool hat and boots. He says he is from Harford and is free. He is somewhat deranged in mind. If not claimed, he will be discharged according to law.

ROBERT M. WALMSLEY, Sheriff.

sept. 2—3t.

Crummill, James. "June 2/55. James Crummill, Sam'l. Jones, Tolburt Jones & Henry Howard arrived safely [into Philadelphia] from Ladies Manor, Haverford Co, Md. [My Lady's Manor, Harford County]. James had been owned by Wm. Hutchins, so had Saml. & Tolbert belonged to the same master, Hutchins. They said their owner was a very hard master, frollicing, &c. Henry had been owned by Phillip Garrison. Lived Hutchins Farm. Since the death of the old master, he had seen ruff usage. His master had been threatened *(sic)* to sell him south frequently. All of the 4 are of medium size, quite above average in point of intilect and seem intell[igent] to be of sobour temperament. Left on Wis

[Whitsuntide]. James Crummill left a wife, free, named Charlotte. She was privey to her husband's leaving." (Ref: *Journal C of Station No. 2 of the Underground Railroad, Agent William Still, 1852-1857.* Vigilance Committee of Philadelphia, Pennsylvania Anti-Slavery Society, Pennsylvania Abolition Society Papers, Historical Society of Pennsylvania); see Negro James.

Curtis, Mary E. "Runaway. Was committed to the jail of Harford County, on the 23rd of October last [1860]. a Negro Woman who calls herself Mary E. Curtis, aged about 30 years, a bright mulatto, about 5 feet 5 or 6 inches high, as a runaway. The owner (if any) is requested to call on the sheriff, or she will be disposed of according to law. Joseph E. Bateman, Sheriff." (Ref: *Southern Aegis*, 1 Dec 1860)

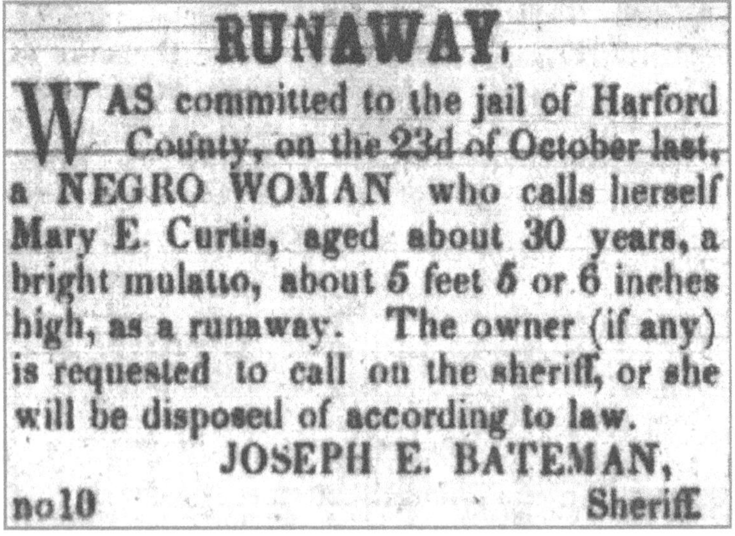

RUNAWAY.

WAS committed to the jail of Harford County, on the 23d of October last, a NEGRO WOMAN who calls herself Mary E. Curtis, aged about 30 years, a bright mulatto, about 5 feet 5 or 6 inches high, as a runaway. The owner (if any) is requested to call on the sheriff, or she will be disposed of according to law.

JOSEPH E. BATEMAN,

no10 Sheriff.

Curtus, Nead. "Know all men by these presents that I Josias Mathews of Harford County and State of Maryland do hereby make, constitute and appoint Thomas Shay of

County & State aforesaid my true and lawfull attorney for me and in my name to ask, demand, sue for recover, apprehend, and take up, my runaway slave where ever he may be found, viz. my negro man Nead (alias Nead Curtus) and him to lodged in goal [jail] or bring him on to me in said County as to the said Thomas Shay may be most convenient. In witness whereof I have hereunto set my hand and seal this tenth day of June in the year one thousand eight hundred and twelve. Josiah Mathews. Signed, sealed and delivered in the presence of Henry Vansickle, Bened. [Benedict] H. Hanson." (Ref: Historical Society of Harford County, Archives File "Slavery – Runaways")

Damon, Jane. "$100 Reward. – Ran away on the 3rd inst. [1859], a Negro Woman named Jane Damon. She is about 18 years old, very dark, about 5 feet 4 inches high, pleasant when spoken to. The above reward will be given for her return to Wm. Hughes, Jarrettsville, Harford co., Md." (Ref: *Baltimore Sun*, 6 Apr 1859)

Dawson, Peter. "Four Pounds Reward. Ran away, on the 1st of June inst. [1789] two negro men, the one about 5 feet 7 or 8 inches high, about 24 years of age, can speak the German language, being bred amongst the Dutch [Deutsch, meaning German], speaks broken English, chews tobacco, which makes his teeth blackish, and called himself Peter Dawson; had on, when he went away, a felt hat, old light coloured great coat, a brown fustian straight cost, tow shirt and trowsers dyed brown, linsey jacket with broad deep blue stripes, and old shoes; was born in West Jersey, on the Delaware, and it is likely will try for that place. The other a well-made fellow, named Daniel, a shoemaker by trade, speaks good English, his cloathing not known. Whoever takes up and secures the above Negroes, so as the owner may have them again, shall have the above reward, or Two Pounds for each, and reasonable charges, paid by the subscriber, living near Haverdegrass [Havre de Grace], Harford County, State of Maryland. William Luckie." (Ref: *The Pennsylvania Gazette*, 10 Jun 1789)

Demby, Harriet. "$600 Reward. – Ran away from the subscribers' Farms, in Harford County, on Saturday night, September 3rd [1842], the following described Negroes: Harriet Demby, 23 years old, colour black, thick lips, forehead full, very small hands and small feet and ears, wool fine, and when well combed nearly straight, a little below medium stature, speaks low. Among her clothing were four Calico dresses, various colours, a black and white Straw Bonnet trimmed with pea green ribbon, a cross-bar scarlet and green Blanket Shawl, Worked Collars, Capes and Wrist Cuffs. Hull Rice, 28 years old, colour black, medium stature, very erect, pleasant address, very little beard, lisps slightly. The above Negroes were engaged to be married, and now, doubtless, live together as Man and Wife. George Stewart, 28 years old, dark Mulatto or copper colour, below medium stature, small head, awkward form and manner, short Negro hair, and very little beard, speaks remarkably quick. The above Slaves have probably crossed the Susquehanna River at some point between Port Deposite [actually Deposit] and Columbia Bridge. We will give $200 for the apprehension of either or the same sum for each. Charles W. Lee, Churchville, Harford County, Md. Josiah Lee, Baltimore." (Ref: *Baltimore American and Commercial Daily Advertiser*, 7 Sep 1842)

Dixon, Ben. "Five Hundred Dollars Reward. Ran away from the subscribers, living near Joppa, Harford County, Md., on Saturday, 28th of July last [1841], Three Negro

Men, calling themselves Phil Dixon, Ben Dixon, and Jack Parks. Phil is about 35 years old, 5 feet 10 inches high, of a corpulent make, very dark, has a dull speech, and has lost some of his front teeth. Ben is about 30 years old, 5 feet 8 or 9 inches high, of a slender appearance, pleasant address, and very polite when spoken to. Jack is about 40 years old, 5 feet 10 or 11 inches high, has a pleasant appearance when spoken to, and is very dark. The above reward will be given for the apprehension of the above negroes, or a proportional reward for either, if taken within this State or elsewhere, and lodged in jail so that the owners may get them again. C. W. Hatton. Catherine Parks." (Ref: *Baltimore Sun*, 6 Sep 1841)

Dixon, Phil. "Five Hundred Dollars Reward. Ran away from the subscribers, living near Joppa, Harford County, Md., on Saturday, 28th of July last [1841], Three Negro Men, calling themselves Phil Dixon, Ben Dixon, and Jack Parks. Phil is about 35 years old, 5 feet 10 inches high, of a corpulent make, very dark, has a dull speech, and has lost some of his front teeth. Ben is about 30 years old, 5 feet 8 or 9 inches high, of a slender appearance, pleasant address, and very polite when spoken to. Jack is about 40 years old, 5 feet 10 or 11 inches high, has a pleasant appearance when spoken to, and is very dark. The above reward will be given for the apprehension of the above negroes, or a proportional reward for either, if taken within this State or elsewhere, and lodged in jail so that the owners may get them again. C. W. Hatton. Catherine Parks." (Ref: *Baltimore Sun*, 6 Sep 1841)

Forwood, Dan. "Two Hundred Dollars Reward. – Ran away from the subscriber, living in Bush River Neck, a Negro Man, who calls himself Dan Forwood. He is about 5 feet 8 or 10 inches high, and rather stout made; his features are rather short; and when spoken to so as to embarrass him, stammers very much as though he would choke. He has no marks on him that are recollected, except on one of his arms or near the elbow, occasioned by a burn. The said man is about 20 years of age. He took with him one pair of coarse boots, double soled and nailed, nearly new – also, one pair [of] coarse shoes, nailed and nearly new – also, one blue cassinet roundabout jacket, one swansdown vest, besides other clothing not recollected. The above reward will be paid if the said Negro is brought home, or lodged in any Jail so that I get him again, and all reasonable charges paid. Richard Kenly." (Ref: *Baltimore Sun*, 14 Oct 1841)

TWO HUNDRED DOLLARS REWARD.—Ranaway from the subscriber, living in Bush River Neck, a NEGRO MAN, who calls himself DAN FORWOOD. He is about 5 feet 8 or 10 inches high, and rather stout made; his features are rather short; and when spoken to so as to embarrass him, stammers very much as though he would choke. He has no marks on him that are recollected, except on one of his arms or near the elbow, occasioned by a burn. The said man is about 20 years of age. He took with him one pair of coarse boots, double soled and nailed, nearly new—also, one pair coarse shoes, nailed and nearly new—also, one blue cassinet roundabout jacket; one swansdown vest, besides other clothing not recollected. The above reward will be paid if the said Negro is brought home, or lodged in any Jail so that I get him again, and all reasonable charges paid. RICHARD KENLY. o14-3t

Francis, Lewis. "One Hundred Dollars Reward. Absconded from the farm of the late Francis Delmas, near Abingdon, Harford County, Md., on the 22nd ult. [May

1846] a Negro Slave, belonging to the estate of said F. Delmas, named Lewis Francis. He is about 40 years of age, 5 feet 5 inches high, and has lost some of his front teeth. He was last seen in company with several other blacks on their way to Havre de Grace. The above reward will be paid by the subscriber to anyone who will bring back said slave, or secure him in any County jail in the State. E. Laroque, Ex'r of Francis Delmas, dec'd. [Harford Madisonian, Havre de Grace, Md., copy to the amount of $1 and send bill to advertiser.]" (Ref: *Baltimore Sun*, 3 Jun 1846)

Frederick, William. "One Hundred Dollars Reward. – Ran away from the subscriber, living in Harford County, Md., on the 23rd [of] May [1846], a Negro Man, who calls himself William Frederick. The said fellow is about thirty-five years old; five feet six or eight inches in height; sturdy and well made; stoops a little in his shoulders. The most remarkable feature in the description of said fellow is that he is blind in one of his eyes, believed to be the right eye. Fifty dollars reward will be given for the apprehension of said fellow if taken within the State, and the above reward if taken without the State, and confined in some jail so that I get him again. Horatio D. Strong." (Ref: *Baltimore Sun*, 27 May 1846). [Horatio Day Strong (1812-1853), and wife Catherine S. (Nabb) Strong, lived in the Third District.]

Gibbs, William Henry. "$25 Reward. – Ran away from the subscriber, on Wednesday, 12th inst. [November 1845] from the team on the road to Baltimore, near the first gate on the Harford Road, a Negro Boy by the name of Wm. Henry Smith, alias Gibbs, between 18 and 19 years old, 5 feet 9 or 10 inches high, copper color, and had on an old fur cap, red and drab coat and new home-made pants. The above reward will be paid for his return to me, near

Jarrettsville, Harford County, or lodged in jail so that I may get him again. Shedrach Street." (Ref: *Baltimore Sun*, 13 Nov 1845)

Gittings, Jim. "$100 Reward. Ran away from the late residence of Benjamin Buck, dec'd., in Baltimore County, on Sunday night, 29th October [1837], a negro man named Jim, belonging to the estate of said Buck – calls himself Jim Gittings. He is about 33 years of age, 5 feet 7 or 8 inches high, stout built, black, and has a pleasant countenance, no particular marks about him that are recollected. Had on when he went away, black cloth coat and fulled linzy pants, and took a quantity of other clothing, principally drab cloth.

"Jim took with him a fine black mare, about 10 years old, 14 or 15 hands high, with a star on her forehead, Fifty dollars will be given for the recovery of the negro if taken within the State, or $100 if taken without the limits of the State of Maryland, with all reasonable charges, if brought home, or lodged in jail so that I get him again, and $20 for the recovery of the mare. Henry W. Archer, Receiver. Bel Air, Nov. 9, 1837." (Ref: *The Madisonian and Harford and Baltimore Advertiser*, 7 Dec 1837)

Glover, Jacob. "Thirty Dollars Reward. Ran Away, from the subscriber, on Friday the 27th instant [April 1786], a Mulatto Man, named Jacob Glover, about 50 years of age, 5 feet 6 or 7 inches high, curly hair, somewhat gray, thin visage; he took with him sundry cloaths, among which was a snuff-coloured broad-cloth coat, and a pair of plush breeches. He is a tanner and currier by trade, but has for some years attended a mill. He pretends to be knowing in farrying [horse shoeing] and keeping race-horses, which is probably the business he will wish to follow. Any person apprehending said fellow, and delivering him to the subscriber, shall have, if taken in the County, Eight Dollars; if out of the County and 30 miles from home, Ten Dollars; if 40 miles, Twelve Dollars, and so in proportion; but if upwards of 100 miles from home, the above reward, paid by me Edward Hall. Cranbury, Harford County, Maryland, April 29, 1786. N.B. All matters of vessels are forewarned from carrying off said Runaway, as they will answer it at their peril." (Ref: *Maryland Journal and Baltimore Advertiser*, 5 Aug 1786)

Thirty Dollars Reward.

RAN AWAY, from the ſubſcriber, on Friday the 27th inſtant, a *Mulatto Man*, named *JACOB GLOVER*, about 50 years of age, 5 feet 6 or 7 inches high, curly hair, ſomewhat gray, thin viſage; he took with him ſundry cloaths, among which are a ſnuff-coloured broad-cloth coat, and a pair of pluſh breeches. He is a tanner and currier by trade, but has for ſome years attended a mill. He pretends to be knowing in farrying and keeping race-horſes, which is probably the buſineſs he will wiſh to follow. Any perſon apprehending ſaid fellow, and delivering him to the ſubſcriber, ſhall have, if taken in the County, Eight Dollars; if out of the County and 30 miles from home, Ten Dollars; if 40 miles, Twelve Dollars, and ſo in proportion; but if upwards of 100 miles from home, the above Reward, paid by me

EDWARD HALL.

Cranbury, Harford County, Maryland, April, 29, 1786.

N. B. All maſters of veſſels are forewarned from carrying off ſaid Runaway, as they will anſwer it at their peril.

Green, Bill. "Was Committed to the Jail of Harford County, on the 18th day of August, 1862, as a runaway, a Negro Boy who calls himself Bill Green. He is about 12 years of age, is 4 feet 5 inches high. He had on when committed a black cap and light pants. This said negro was committed to the Jail of Harford County, Maryland, as a runaway. The owner (if any) of the above-described negro is requested to come forward, prove property, pay charges, and take him away; otherwise, he will be disposed of according to the Act of Assembly, in such cases made and provided. Charles D. Bouldin, Sheriff. (Ref: *National American*, 29 Aug 1862)

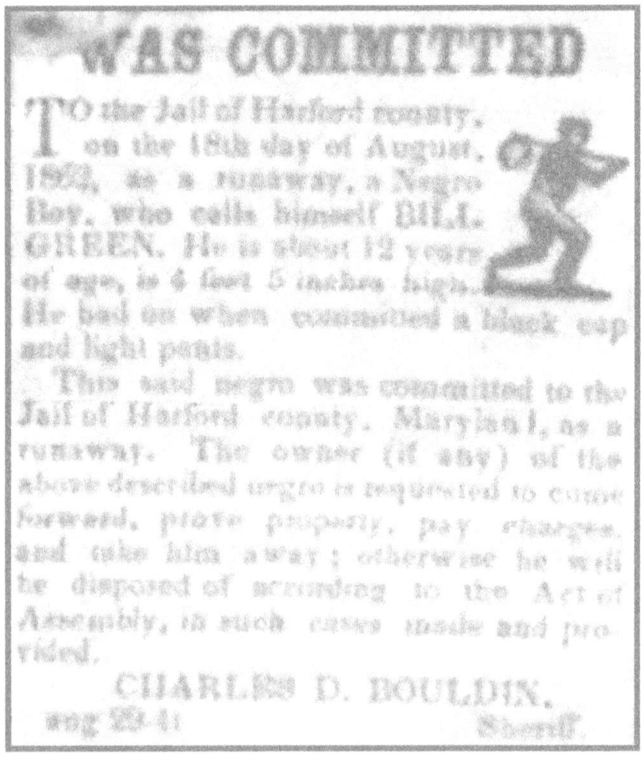

WAS COMMITTED

TO the Jail of Harford county, on the 18th day of August, 1862, as a runaway, a Negro Boy, who calls himself BILL GREEN. He is about 12 years of age, is 4 feet 5 inches high. He had on when committed a black cap and light pants.

This said negro was committed to the Jail of Harford county, Maryland, as a runaway. The owner (if any) of the above described negro is requested to come forward, prove property, pay charges, and take him away; otherwise he will be disposed of according to the Act of Assembly, in such cases made and provided.

CHARLES D. BOULDIN,

aug 29-4t Sheriff.

Haley, Harriet. "Harriet Haley, alias Ann Richardson, and Elizabeth Haley, alias Sarah Richardson [1854]. These travelers succeeded in escaping from Geo. C. Davis, of Harford County, Md. In order to carry out their plans, they took advantage of Whitsuntide, a holiday, and with marked ingenuity and perseverance, they managed to escape and reach Quakertown [PA] Underground Rail Road Station without obstruction, where protection and assistance were rendered by the friends of the cause. After abiding there for a short time, they were forwarded to the Committee in Philadelphia. Their ages ranged from nineteen to twenty-one, and they were apparently 'servants' of a very superior order. The pleasure is afforded to aid such young women in escaping from a condition so loathsome as that of Slavery in Maryland, was unalloyed." (Ref: *The Underground Rail-road*, by William Still, 1871, repr. 1970, pp. 229-230)

"Since coming into the state [they] have been living in Quakertown where they were much respected & parted with regret. Ann is about 19 & Sarah 21 yrs of age, both very nice-looking girls. Boarding, Carriage & Telegraph Dispatch, $2.25." (Ref: *Journal C of Station No. 2 of the Underground Railroad, Agent William Still, 1852-1857.* Vigilance Committee of Philadelphia, Pennsylvania Anti-Slavery Society, Pennsylvania Abolition Society Papers, Historical Society of Pennsylvania)

Hall, Abraham. "Philadelphia, Sept. 17. [1851]. Fugitive Slave Surrendered. – On Monday afternoon, Abraham Hall was arrested by some police officers from Lancaster, as the alleged fugitive slave of John Slade, of Harford County, Md. He was found in the mountains some few miles from Christiana, and last evening was in custody at that place. Two persons from Maryland identified Hall, who had run off about three years since. Today he was surrendered to his owner. He expressed a strong desire to return home." (Ref: *Harford Madisonian and Havre de Grace Weekly Adver-tiser*, 18 Sep 1851)

"*The Fugitive Slave Case* ... U.S. Commissioner Ingraham is now engaged in hearing a fugitive slave case.

The colored man claimed was named Abraham Hall, who five years since ran away from John Slade, of Harford County, Md. He fled in consequence of having beaten a grandson of his master, in a sudden fit of passion. Since that time, he has been living in Lancaster County by the name of Charles Givin. He admits being a runaway, and expresses a willingness to go back, but the abolitionists made an effort to free him from the claim. The evidence was, however, convincing, and he has been remanded unto the custody of his owner, and will go home by the afternoon boat." (Ref: *Baltimore Sun*, 18 Sep 1851; *National Era*, 25 Sep 1851)

PHILADELPHIA, Sept. 17.

Fugitive Slave Surrendered.—On Monday afternoon, Abraham Hall was arrested by some police officers from Lancaster, as the alleged fugitive slave of John Slade, of Harford county, Md.—He was found in the mountains some few miles from Christiana, and last evening was in custody at that place. Two persons from Maryland identified Hall, who had ran off about three years since. To day he was surrendered to his owner. He expressed a strong desire to return home.

Harriss, William. "Notice – as committed to my jail and custody as a runaway, on the 30th day of May last [1810], a negro man who calls himself William Harriss, about 23 years old, 5 feet 8 or 9 inches high, has a pleasant countenance, quick speech, very white and regular teeth. His clothing consists of a dark grey cloth surtout coat, a waistcoat of yellow and white striped Marseilles, a pair of corduroy pantaloons and old felt hat and a pair of old shoes, says he served an apprenticeship of four years with Joseph Priggs [actually Prigg] of Harford County, state of Maryland, to the shoe-making business. The owner is requested to come forward, pay charges, and take him away, or he will be sold for his prison fees as the law directs. John Darnall, Sheriff of Prince George's County." (Ref: *National Intelligencer and Washington Advertiser*, 6 Jul 1810)

Heath, Charles. "Runaway Slaves. – On Saturday night last [25 Jun 1859] some eight or nine slaves ran away from their owners at Perrymansville and that vicinity. Three of them belonged to A. D. Keen, Esq." (Ref: *Baltimore Sun*, 2 Jul 1859)

"Arrival from Maryland [into Philadelphia]. Jim Kell, Charles Heath, William Carlisle, Charles Ringgold, Thomas Maxwell, and Samuel Smith. Charles Heath had had his head cut shockingly, with a club, in the hands of his master; this well-cared for individual in referring to his kind *(sic)* master: 'I can give his character right along, he was a perfect devil. The night we left, he had a woman tied up – God knows what he done. He was always blustering; you could never do enough for him no how. First thing in the morning and last thing at night, you would hear him cussing – he would cuss in bed. He was a large farmer, all the time drunk. He had a good deal of money, but not much character. He was a savage, bluff, red face-looking concern.' Thus, in the most earnest, we well as in intelligent manner, Charles described the man (Aquila Cain), who had hitherto held him under the yoke ... Charles Heath was twenty-five years of age, medium size, full black, a very keen-looking individual … After being furnished with food clothing, and free tickets, they were forwarded on in triumph and full of hope." [While in bondage] "Charles had

had five men on him at one time, with cowhides, his master in the lead." (Ref: *The Underground Railroad*, by William Still, 1871, repr. 1970, pp. 521-522).

The services of Charles Heath, age 26 in 1852, were sold to Aquila and B. H. Keen by Timothy Keen in 1852 for $400 "until freed in ten years at age 36." [It would have occurred in 1862 if he had not successfully escaped in 1859.] (Ref: *Hunter Sutherland's Slave Manumissions and Sales in Harford County, Maryland, 1775-1865*, by Carolyn Greenfield Adams, 1999, p. 94)

Henly, William H. "Five Dollars Reward. – Ran away on the 25th of April last [1838], from the subscriber, living near the Upper Cross Roads in Harford County, a bound Mulatto Boy, by the name of William H. Henly, about fourteen years old. His hair does not curl, but it is straight, very coarse and black; his eyes are of a grayish blue; has a small wen [cyst] on one of his eye brows. The above reward will be paid to anyone who may deliver him to me, or secure him in jail, so that I get him again. Joshua Amos." (Ref: *Baltimore Sun*, 14 Dec 1838)

> FIVE DOLLARS REWARD.—Ranaway on the 25th of April last, from the subscriber, living near the Upper Cross Roads in Harford county, a bound MULATTO BOY, by the name of WILLIAM H. HENLY, about fourteen years old. His hair does not curl, but it is straight, very coarse and black; his eyes are of a grayish blue; has a small wen on one of his eye brows. The above reward will be paid to any one who may deliver him to me, or secure him in jail, so that I get him again.
>
> d14 3t* JOSHUA AMOS.

Henson, Thomas, George, Lloyd, and Andrew. "Four Hundred Dollars Reward. Ran away from the subscribers, residing in Harford County, Md., on the 23rd inst. [May 1846], Negro Man, who calls himself Thomas Henson. The said fellow is about thirty years old, about five feet four or five inches high, sturdy and well made, of a dark complexion and a downcast look when spoken to. The said boy had on when he started, a plaid coat, green cloth pants, and a cloth and fur hat, but which he had doubtless changed, as he took with him a variety. Also, a Negro Man, who calls himself Geo. Henson; aged about twenty-five years, about five feet six inches high and well made, dark complexion, considerable beard, and is rather pleasant when spoken to. Also, a Negro Boy, who calls himself Lloyd Henson, aged about twenty years, about five feet high and well made, about five feet high and well made, dark complexion, and rather sullen in his manner. Also, a [Negro] boy, who calls himself Andrew Henson, aged about eighteen years, about five feet three or four inches high, rather spare in his make, complexion dark, full face, and down look when spoken to. Fifty Dollars reward will be given for the apprehension of each or either of the above boys if taken within the State, and the above reward of One Hundred Dollars a piece if taken without the State, and confined in some jail, so that we get them again. The abovementioned boys are brothers. John Chisholm. Chas. Chisholm." (Ref: *Baltimore Sun*, 27 May 1846)

Hewitt, Thomas. "Five Cents Reward. Ran Away from the subscriber, on the 2nd instant [2 Mar 1863], Thomas Hewitt, a bright Mulatto Boy, 17 years old, light built, decayed front teeth. All persons are hereby warned not to harbor or employ said boy. The above reward will be paid any one who will return him to F. Whitaker." (Ref: *The Southern*

Aegis, 13 Mar 1863). [F. Whitaker was Franklin Whitaker (1818-1891), owner of Whitaker's Mill on Winter's Run.]

Five Cents Reward!

RAN AWAY from the subscriber, on the 2d instant, THOMAS HEWITT, a bright Mulatto Boy, 17 years old, light built, decayed front teeth. All persons are hereby warned not to harbor or employ said boy.

The above reward will be paid any one who will return him to

mh13 F. WHITAKER.

Hill, George. "Arrival from Arlington [Darlington], MD [into Philadelphia], 1857. John Alexander Butler, William Henry Hipkins, John Henry Moore and George Hill. This party made, at first sight, a favorable impression; they represented the bone and sinew of the slave class of Arlington *(sic)*, and upon investigation the Committee felt assured that they would carry with them to Canada industry and determination such as would tell well for the race.

"George Hill, also a fellow passenger, was about twenty-four years of age, quite black, medium size, and of fair, natural mother wit. In looking back upon his days of bondage, his mind reverted to Dr. Savington [actually Dr. John Sappington, 1801-1869], of Harford County, as the person who owed him for years of hard and unrequited toil, and at the same time was his so-called owner.

"The Doctor, it seemed, had failed to treat George well, for he declared that he had never received enough to eat the whole time that he was with him. 'The clothes I have on I got by overwork of nights. When I started I hadn't a shoe on my foot, these were given to me. He was an old man, but a very wicked man, and drank very hard.' George had been taught field work pretty thoroughly, but nothing in the way of reading and writing.

"George explained why he left as follow: 'I left because I had got along with him as well as I could. Last Saturday a week he was in a great rage and drunk. He shot at me. He never went away but what he would come home drunk, and if anybody made him angry out from home, he would come home and take his spite out of his people.' He owned three grown men, two women and six children. Thus, hating Slavery heartily, George was enthusiastically in favor of Canada.

"When [the] charges or statements were made by fugitives against those from whom they escaped, particular pains were taken to find out if such statements could be verified; if the explanation appeared valid, the facts as given were entered on the books." (Ref: *The Underground Railroad*, by William Still, 1871, repr. 1970, pp. 434-435); *A Journey Through Berkley, Maryland*, by Constance R. Beims and Christine P. Tolbert, 2003, pp. 45-46)

Hill, John. 1778. In describing the escape of Negro London [aka Daniel Anderson] from the jail in New Castle Co., DE, it was reported: "Likewise, a Mulatto fellow named John Hill, a Methodist preacher, formerly lived in Charlestown, Maryland; he passed the above Negro for a free man at Capt. Ellis at the Head of the Bohemia [Cecil County], and it is thought he harbours in Hartford *(sic)* County. Whoever secures said Mulatto in any gaol, so that he may be brought to justice, and gives the subscriber notice shall have Thirty Dollars reward and reasonable charges, paid by James Young." (Ref: *The Pennsylvania Packet*, 6 Jun 1778)

Hipkins, William Henry. 1857. "Arrival from Arlington [Darlington], MD [to Philadelphia]. John Alexander Butler,

William Henry Hipkins, John Henry Moore and George Hill. "This party made at first sight, a favorable impression; they represented the bone and sinew of the slave class of Arlington *(sic)*, and upon investigation the Committee felt assured that they would carry with them to Canada industry and determination such as would tell well for the race. William Henry, who was heart and soul in earnest with regard to reaching Canada, and was one of this party, was twenty-three years of age, and was a stout, yellow man with a remarkably large head, and looked as if he was capable of enjoying Canada and caring for himself.

'In speaking of the fettered condition from which he had escaped, the name of Ephraim Swart, 'a gambler and spree'r, was mentioned as the individual who had wronged him of his liberty most grievously.

"Against Swart he expressed himself with much manly feeling, and judging from his manner he appeared to be a dangerous customer for master Swart to encounter north of Mason and Dixon's line.

"William complained that Swart would come home late at night drunk, and if he did not find us awake, he would not attempt to wake us, but would begin cutting and slashing with a cowhide. He treated his wife very bad too; some-times when she would stand up for the servants, he would knock her down. Many times, at midnight she would have to leave the house and go to her mother for safety; she was a very nice woman, but he was the very old Satan himself.'

"While William Henry was debarred from learning letters under his brutal overseer, he nevertheless learned how to plan ways and means by which to escape his bondage. He left his old mother and two brothers wholly ignorant of his movements … When charges or statements were made by fugitives against those from whom they escaped, particular pains were taken to find out if such statements could be verified; if the explanation appeared valid, the facts as given were entered on the books." (Ref: *The Underground Railroad*, by William Still, 1871, repr. 1970, pp. 434-435); *A Journey Through Berkley, Maryland*, by Constance R. Beims and Christine P. Tolbert, 2003, pp. 45-46).

William Henry Hipkins was born 15 Jun 1834 and was an indentured with the consent of his mother (name not given) to learn to be a farmer (master not named) in 1841. (Ref: Harford County General Entries TSB No. 3, p. 249).

William H. Hopkins, an apprentice, was involved in a legal matter in 1850. (Ref: Historical Society of Harford County, Court Records Document 109.20.10)

Holliday, George. "Ran Away – On Saturday night last [26 Aug 1848], from the Farmers' Hotel, corner of Forest and Hillen streets, Old Town, Baltimore, where he was hired, a dark Mulatto Boy, supposed to be about 16 years, of age, named George Holliday, belonging to Mr. Emmor Woodward, of Harford County. He has taken sundry clothing that I cannot describe, more than a pair of new boots and frock coat. Any person that will stop said boy, will be rewarded by his master, Mr. Emmor Woodward. Jehu Young." (Ref: *Baltimore Sun*, 29 Aug 1848)

"Two Hundred Dollars Reward. – Ran away from the subscriber, on Sunday last, 27th inst. [August 1848], two Negro Boys named George and Jim Holliday. Jim is about 20 years of age, 5 feet 9 inches high; quite black; stout built and as smooth as an eel; had on a white linen coat and striped pants. George is about 16 years of age, 5 feet 4 or 5 inches high; a mulatto; has long hair, and of slender make; his clothing consisted of a casinet frock coat, and he was otherwise well dressed. He has been accustomed to the duty of house servant. These negroes were seen near the Upper Cross-roads, Harford County, it is supposed on their way to Pennsylvania. I will pay the above reward for the recovery of said Negroes, or one hundred dollars for either of them, if secured in jail so that I get them again. Eminor [actually Emmor] Woodward, Upper Cross Roads, Harford Co., Md." (Ref: *Baltimore Sun*, 1 Sep 1848)

Holliday, Jim. "Two Hundred Dollars Reward. – Ran away from the subscriber, on Sunday last, 27th inst. [August 1848], two Negro Boys named George and Jim Holliday. Jim is about 20 years of age, 5 feet 9 inches high; quite black; stout built and as smooth as an eel; had on a white linen coat and striped pants. George is about 16 years of age, 5 feet 4 or 5 inches high; a mulatto; has long hair, and of slender make; his clothing consisted of a casinet frock coat, and he was otherwise well dressed. He has been accustomed to the duty of house servant. These negroes were seen near the Upper Cross-roads, Harford County, it is supposed on their way to Pennsylvania. I will pay the above reward for the recovery of said Negroes, or one hundred dollars for either of them, if secured in jail so that I get them again. Eminor [actually Emmor] Woodward, Upper Cross Roads, Harford Co., Md." (Ref: *Baltimore Sun*, 1 Sep 1848)

Hopkins, Sydney. He escaped to Philadelphia circa 1858 with Henry Wheeler. "These young men made their way out of Slavery together. While Sydney lives, he will forever regard Jacob Hoag, of Havre de Grace, as the person who cheated him out of himself, and prevented him from becoming enlightened and educated." (Ref: *The Underground Railroad*, by William Still, 1871, repr. 1970, p. 514)

Howard, Henry. "June 2/55. James Crummill, Sam'l. Jones, Tolburt Jones & Henry Howard arrived safely [into Philadelphia] from Ladies Manor, Haverford Co, Md. [My Lady's Manor, Harford County]. James had been owned by Wm. Hutchins, so had Saml. & Tolbert belonged to the same master, Hutchins. They said their owner was a very hard master, frollicing, &c. Henry had been owned by Phillip Garrison. Lived Hutchins Farm. Since the death of the old master, he had seen ruff usage. His master had been threatened *(sic)* to sell him south frequently. All of the 4 are of medium size, quite above average in point of intilect and seem intell[igent] to be of sobour temperament. Left on Wis [Whitsuntide]. James Crummill left a wife, free, named Charlotte. She was privey to her husband's leaving." (Ref: *Journal C of Station No. 2 of the Underground Railroad, Agent William Still, 1852-1857.* Vigilance Committee of Philadelphia, Pennsylvania Anti-Slavery Society, Pennsylvania Abolition Society Papers, Historical Society of Pennsylvania; *The Underground Railroad Authentic Narratives and First-Hand Accounts*, by William Still, 1872, repr. 2007, p. 160)

Jackson, James. This mulatto man was held in the jail of Harford County on suspicion of being a runaway and was discharged by order of the court on 13 Aug 1808. (Ref: Harford County Court Minutes, 1807-1815)

Johnson, Charles. "$200 Reward. – Ran away from the subscriber on the 27th inst. [September 1840], a Negro Boy named Charles Johnson, nineteen years old, five feet eight or ten inches high, well made, of down look when spoken too *(sic)*, skin not very black, had on when he went away blue cassinett pants and roundabout, striped silk vest and black fur hat. I will give one hundred dollars if taken in the

State, or the above reward if taken out of the State, and secured in any Jail, so I get him. All reasonable expenses paid if brought home. James Maxwell, Near Michaelsville, Harford County, Md." (Ref: *Baltimore American*, 2 Oct 1840)

$200 REWARD.—Ranaway from the subscriber on the 27th inst., a Negro Boy named CHARLES JOHNSON, nineteen years old, five feet eight or ten inches high, well made, of down look when spoken too, skin not very black, had on when he went away blue cassinett pants and roundabout, striped silk vest and black fur hat. I will give one hundred dollars if taken in the State, or the above reward if taken out of the State, and secued in any Jail, so I get him. All reasonable expenses paid if brought home. JAMES MAXWELL,

Near Michaelsville, Harford County,

oc 2 2aw4t* Maryland.

Johnson, Dinah. "20 Dollars Reward. – Ran away on the 19th instant [1831], a bright mulatto girl named Dinah Johnson, 21 years of age, and lame of the left leg; she has broad flat features and eyes turned up at the temples. The above reward will be given for securing said runaway so I may get her again, and the penalties of the law will be enforced against anyone found harbouring her. E. Raphel, Harford County, Dec. 22-26." (Ref: *Baltimore American and Commercial Daily Advertiser*, 26 Dec 1831)

Johnson, Frank. "Was Committed To the Jail of Harford County, on the 18th day of August, 1862, as a runaway, a Negro Boy, who calls himself Frank Johnson. He is about 13 years of age, is 4 feet 6 inches high, is smart and intelligent. He had on when committed a black jacket, no sleeves, and nankeen pants. The said negro was committed to the Jail of Harford County, Maryland, as a runaway. The owner (if any) of the above-described negro is requested to come forward, prove property, pay charges, and take him away; otherwise, he will be disposed of according to the Act of Assembly, in such cases make and provided. Charles D. Bouldin, Sheriff." (Ref: *National American*, 29 Aug 1862). [This may be the Frank Johnson, age about 10 in 1860 who was enumerated in the household of Hedges Matthews. (Ref: 1860 Harford County Census)]

Johnson, Henry. "Two Thousand Dollars Reward. – The above reward will be paid for the apprehension of four blacks, who escaped on Sunday last [31 May 1857]. It is supposed they have made their way to Pennsylvania. $500 will be paid for the apprehension of either, so that we can get them again. Henry Johnson is a colored negro, about 5 feet seven or eight inches high; aged 19 years; has a pleasant countenance, and has a mark on his neck below the ear." (Ref: *Baltimore Sun*, 5 Jun 1857)

"From the Underground Railroad Records. The following memorandum is made, which, if not too late, may afford some light to 'Elizabeth Brown and Thomas Johnson,' if they have not already gone the way of the 'lost cause.' Henry Johnson is a colored negro, about five feet seven or eight inches high, heavily made, aged nineteen years. Has a pleasant countenance, and has a mark on his neck below the ear ... The clothing not recollected. They had black frock coats and slouch hats with them. Any information of them, address Elizabeth Brown, Sandy Hook P. O., or of Thomas Johnson, Abingdon P. O, Harford County, Md." (Ref: *The Underground Railroad Authentic Narratives and First-Hand Accounts*, by William Still, 1872, repr. 2007, p. 40). A later entry stated: "Henry is of a brown skin, a good-looking young man, only nineteen years of age, whose prepossessing appearance would insure a high price for him in the market – perhaps $1,700. With Edward [Morgan] he testifies to the meanness of Mrs. Betsy Brown, as well as his own longing desire for freedom. Being a fellow servant with Edward, Henry was a party to the plan of escape. In slavery he left his mother and three sisters, owned by the 'old woman' from whom he escaped." (Ref: *The Underground Railroad Authentic Narratives and First-Hand Accounts*, by William Still, 1872, repr. 2007, p. 41)

Johnson, James. 1856. "Apr. 9th arrived [into Philadelphia] from Deer Creek, Harford Co., Md, where he had been owned by Wm. Rantly [Ramply?]. The day before James fled was the day fixed for his owner sought to secure him with handcuffs the day before he was to be sold. A determined James fled still shackled to the restraints." (Ref: *Journal C of Station No. 2 of the Underground Railroad, Agent William Still, 1852-1857.* Vigilance Committee of Philadelphia, Pennsylvania Anti-Slavery Society, Pennsylvania Abolition Society Papers, Historical Society of Pennsylvania; Still's *Underground Railroad*, 1870, p. 383)

Johnson, John. "Four Hundred Dollars Reward – Ran away from the subscriber, in Harford County, on Easter Sunday [18 Apr 1858], a black boy, named John Johnson, aged twenty-one years, about six feet high and stout made; has broad front teeth and wide apart. He wore away a gray cloth coat and cap. The above reward will be given if secured and brought to me. Jas. K. Scarff, Jarrettsville, Harford County, Md." (Ref: *Baltimore Sun*, 22 Apr 1858)

Johnson, Nelson. "July 17th 1854. Arrived [in Philadelphia] Nelson Johnson, now Jackson Hall – dark –

medium size – active & about 25 years of age. He was owned by Isaac Stansberry [Stansbury] of Eadens [Eden] Mills, Deer Creek, Hanford [Harford] Co., Md. He had been treated hard. His owner had threatened to sell him only but a few days before he escaped – for fear of which he was induced to escape. Wife's name Hannah, child Mary Luisa, 3 years of age. Board .50, Cash $2.50 [equals] $3.00, Bloods stamps .25 [total] $3.25." (Ref: *Journal C of Station No. 2 of the Underground Railroad, Agent William Still, 1852-1857.* Vigilance Committee of Philadelphia, Pennsylvania Anti-Slavery Society, Pennsylvania Abolition Society Papers, Historical Society of Pennsylvania)

Johnson, Rosanna. 1857-1858. "Rosanna Johnson, alias Catharine Brice. The spot that Rosanna looked upon with most dread and where she had suffered as a slave, under a man called Doctor Street [Dr. Abraham J. Streett, 1799-1867], was near Rock [Rocks] of Deer Creek, in Harford County, Maryland.

"In the darkness in which Slavery ordinarily kept the fettered and 'free niggers' it was a considerable length of time ere Rosanna saw how barbarously she and her race were being wronged and ground down – driven to do requited labor – deprived of an education, obliged to receive the cuffs, kicks, and curses of old or young, who might happen to claim a title to them. But when she did see her true condition, she was not content until she found herself on the Underground Rail Road. Rosanna was about thirty years of age, of a dark color, medium stature, and intelligent. She left two brothers and her father behind. The Committee forwarded her on North.

"From Albany, Rose wrote back to inquire after particular friends, and to thank those who had aided her – as follows: Albany, Jan. the 30, 1858. Mrs. William Still: - I sit don to rite you a fue lines in saying hav you herd of John Smith or Bengernin Pina I have cent letters to them but I hav know word from them John Smith was oned by Doker abe Street Benjermin oned by Mary Hawkings I wish to kno if you kno am if you will let me know as swon as you get this. My lov to Mis Still I am much oblige for those articales. My love to mrs george and verry thankful to her Rosean Johnson oned by docter Street when you cend the letter rite it Cend to 63 Gran St in the car of andrue Conningham rite swon dela it no write my name Cathrin Brice. Let me know swon as you can." (Ref: *The Underground Railroad*, by William Still, 1871, repr. 1970, p. 542)

Jones, Samuel. "June 2/55. James Crummill, Sam'l. Jones, Tolburt Jones & Henry Howard arrived safely [into Philadelphia] from Ladies Manor, Haverford Co, Md. [My Lady's Manor, Harford County]. James had been owned by Wm. Hutchins, so had Saml. & Tolbert belonged to the same master, Hutchins. They said their owner was a very hard master, frollicing, &c. Henry had been owned by Phillip Garrison. Lived Hutchins Farm. Since the death of the old master, he had seen ruff usage. His master had been threatened *(sic)* to sell him south frequently. All of the 4 are of medium size, quite above average in point of intilect and seem intell[igent] to be of sobour temperament. Left on Wis [Whitsuntide]. James Crummill left a wife, free, named Charlotte. She was privey to her husband's leaving." (Ref: *Journal C of Station No. 2 of the Underground Railroad, Agent William Still, 1852-1857.* Vigilance Committee of Philadelphia, Pennsylvania Anti-Slavery Society, Pennsylvania Abolition Society Papers, Hist. Soc. of Pennsylvania)

Jones, Tolburt. "June 2/55. James Crummill, Sam'l. Jones, Tolburt Jones & Henry Howard arrived safely [into

Philadelphia] from Ladies Manor, Haverford Co, Md. [My Lady's Manor, Harford County]. James had been owned by Wm. Hutchins, so had Saml. & Tolbert belonged to the same master, Hutchins. They said their owner was a very hard master, frollicing, &c. Henry had been owned by Phillip Garrison. Lived Hutchins Farm. Since the death of the old master, he had seen ruff usage. His master had been threatened *(sic)* to sell him south frequently. All of the 4 are of medium size, quite above average in point of intilect and seem intell[igent] to be of sobour temperament. Left on Wis [Whitsuntide]. James Crummill left a wife, free, named Charlotte. She was privey to her husband's leaving." (Ref: *Journal C of Station No. 2 of the Underground Railroad, Agent William Still, 1852-1857.* Vigilance Committee of Philadelphia, Pennsylvania Anti-Slavery Society, Pennsylvania Abolition Society Papers, Hist. Soc. of Pennsylvania)

Kell, James. "Arrival from Maryland [into Philadelphia], 1859. Jim Kell, Charles Heath, William Carlisle, Charles Ringgold, Thomas Maxwell, and Samuel Smith ... James left his mother, Nancy Kell, two brothers, Robert and Henry, and two sisters, Mary and Annie; all living in the neighborhood whence he fled. Besides these, he had eight brothers and sisters living in Baltimore and elsewhere, under the yoke. He was twenty-four years of age, of a jet [black] color, but of a manly turn. He fled from Thomas Murphy, a farmer, and regular slave-holder ... After being furnished with food clothing, and free tickets, they were forwarded on in triumph and full of hope." [While in bondage] "Jim had been whipped with clubs and switches times without number." (Ref: *The Underground Railroad,* by William Still, 1871, repr. 1970, pp. 521-522). [There was a James Kell who was listed on the criminal docket (charge undetermined) in Harford County in 1856. (Harford

County Criminal Docket Book, 1852-1858)]

Lemmon, John. "Runaway. Was committed to the Jail of Harford County, on Monday 27th July [1845], a Negro man, as a runaway, calling himself John Lemmon; is 5 feet 8 inches high, rather slender made and good looking, straight nose, has a scar on the upper part of the left wrist, said to have been occasioned by a burn. – Had on when committed a blue cloth coat, grey cassinet pants with black stripes, a dark figured worsted vest, check shirt; says he was raised in York County, Va., but is now from Surrey County, Va.; left there in June last, and was born of free parents. The owner or owners of the above-described negro, if any, is requested to come forward, prove property, pay charges and take him away. Henry Richardson, Sheriff. Aug. 19, 1845." (Ref: *Easton Star*, 19 Aug 1845)

Lingum, Abram. "One Hundred Dollars Reward. – Ran away from the subscriber, on the 2nd inst. [February 1852], Abram Lingum, from Harford County, Md., aged 14 years; about 5 feet 5 inches in height; throws his head back when spoken to, in consequence of heaviness of the eye-lids. Had on when he left, drab pantaloons and coat, blue casinet vest and hair cap. The above reward will be given for the return of said boy to John Shaw, Shawsville, Harford County, Md., or any information that I may get him." (Ref: *Baltimore Sun*, 11 Feb 1852)

Marshel, Sauntee. "100 Dollars Reward. Ran-away from the subscriber, living in Harford County, three miles from Belle-Air, on Monday, 30th July [1810], a negro man named Sauntee, who calls himself Sauntee Marshel, between 24 and 25 years of age, about five feet six or seven inches high; of a yellow complexion; slow speech; wide mouth;

good teeth; flat nose, and a smiling shy countenance when spoken to; one of his fingers on the left hand crooked, occasioned by a hurt in the middle joint of the finger; he also has a knot swelled on one of his wrists, about the size of a robin's egg, near the joint; a very small beard, wears his hair tied behind; and bends somewhat back; had on a ticklenburg shirt and trousers, and a dark striped vest; his other clothing not recollected. The above reward will be paid for the said negro if taken out of the State, fifty dollars if taken out of the County, and twenty dollars if taken in the County, and reasonable charges of brought home, paid by William H. Sewall." (Ref: *Daily National Intelligencer*, 23 Aug 1810)

100 DOLLARS REWARD.

Ran-away from the subscriber, living in Harford County, three miles from Belle-Air, on Monday, 30th July, a *negro man*, named SAUNTEE, who calls himself SAUNTEE M[illegible], between 24 and 25 years of [illegible] about five feet six or seven inches high; of a yellow complexion; slow speech; wide mouth; good teeth; flat nose, and a smiling shy countenance when spoken to; one of his fingers on the left hand crooked, occasioned by a hurt in the middle joint of the finger; he also has a knot swelled on one of his wrists, about the size of a robin's egg, near the joint; a very small beard, wears his hair tied behind; and bends somewhat back; had on a ticklenburg shirt and trousers, and a dark striped vest; his other clothing not recollected.

The above reward will be paid for the said negro, if taken out of the State; fifty dollars if taken out of the county, and twenty dollars if taken in the county, and reasonable charges if brought home, paid by

WILLIAM H. SEWALL.

august 23 d[illegible]

Maxwell, Thomas. "Arrival from Maryland [into Philadelphia], 1859. Jim Kell, Charles Heath, William Carlisle,

Charles Ringgold, Thomas Maxwell, and Samuel Smith ... Thomas was of pure blood, with a very cheerful, healthy-looking countenance – twenty-one years of age, and was to 'come free' at twenty-five, but he had too much good sense to rely upon the promises of slave-holders in matters of this kind. He too belonged to [Aquila] Cain who, he said, was constantly talking about selling, etc. He left his father and mother. After being furnished with food clothing, and free tickets, they were forwarded on in triumph and full of hope." [While in bondage] "Thomas had been clubbed over his head more times than a few." (Ref: *The Underground Railroad*, by William Still, 1871, repr. 1970, pp. 521-522)

Moore, John Henry. 1857. "Arrival from Arlington [Darlington], MD [to Philadelphia]. John Alexander Butler, William Henry Hipkins, John Henry Moore and George Hill. This party made, at first sight, a favorable impression; they represented the bone and sinew of the slave class of Arlington *(sic)*, and upon investigation the Committee felt assured that they would carry with them to Canada industry and determination such as would tell well for the race. John Henry Moore was about twenty-four years of age, a dark, spare-built man. He named David Mitchell, of Havre de Grace, as the individual above all others who had kept his foot on his neck. Without undertaking to give John Henry's description of Mitchell in full, suffice it to give the following facts: 'Mitchell would go off and get drunk, and come home, and if the slaves had not as much work done as he had tasked them with, he would go to beating them with clubs or anything he could get in his hand. He was a tall, spare-built man, with sandy hair. He had a wife and family, but his wife was not better that he was.' When charges or statements were made by fugitives against those from whom they escaped, particular pains were taken to find out if such statements could be verified; if the explanation appeared valid, facts as given were entered on the books.

"John Henry could not read, but greatly desired to learn, and he looked as though he had a good head for so doing. Before he left there had been some talk of selling him South. This rumor had a marked effect upon John Henry's nervous system; it also expanded his idea touching traveling, the Underground Rail Road, etc. As he had brothers and sisters who had been sold to Georgia, he made up his mind that his master was not to be trusted for a single day; he was therefore one of the most willing-hearted passengers in the party." (Ref: *The Underground Railroad*, by William Still, 1871, repr. 1970, pp. 433-434; *A Journey Through Berkley, Maryland*, by Constance R. Beims and Christine P. Tolbert, 2003, pp. 45-46)

Morgan, Edward. "Two Thousand Dollars Reward. – The above reward will be paid for the apprehension of four blacks, who escaped on Sunday last [31 May 1857]. It is supposed they have made their way to Pennsylvania. $500 will be paid for either, so that we can get them again. The oldest is named Edward Morgan, about five feet six or seven [high], heavily made – is a dark black, has rather a down look when spoken to, and is about 21 years of age … The clothing [was] not recollected. They had black frock coats and slouch hats with them. Any information of them, address Elizabeth Brown, Sandy Hook P.O., or of Thomas Johnson, Abingdon P. O., Harford County, Md." (Ref: *Baltimore Sun*, 5 Jun 1857)

"From the Underground Rail Road Records. The following memorandum is made, which, if not too late, may afford some light to 'Elizabeth Brown and Thomas Johnson,' if they have not already gone the way of the 'lost cause.' June 4, 1857 – Edward is a hardy and firm-looking young man of twenty-four years of age, chestnut color, medium size, and 'likely' – would doubtless bring $1,400 in the market. He had been held as the property of the widow, 'Betsy Brown,' who resided near Mill Green P. O., in Harford County, Md. She was a very bad woman; would go to church every Sunday, come home and go to fighting amongst the colored people; was never satisfied; she treated my mother very hard (said Ed.); would beat her with a walking-stick, &c. She was an old woman and belonged to the Catholic Church. Over her slaves she kept an overseer, who was a very wicked man, very bad on colored people; his name was 'Bill Eddy;' Elizabeth Brown owned twelve head." (Ref: *The Underground Railroad Authentic Narratives and First-Hand Accounts*, by William Still, 1872, repr. 2007, pp. 40-41)

Morgan, Margaret. Born in the Mill Green area along Broad Creek circa 1800-1805, her parents had been freed by John Ashmore, but no documents exist to prove it. Margaret married a local free black named Jerry Morgan in 1828 and therefore thought she was also free. They had two children before moving north into neighboring York County in 1832 and there they had four more children. Margaret "Peg" Morgan was the mother of Hester, Lucy, Charles, Elizabeth, Amanda and Margaret Morgan. In 1837 the heirs of John Ashmore wanted to reclaim Margaret Morgan and her offspring. They hired slave hunters and her case led to a Supreme Court case that is summarized herein. Whatever eventually became of Margaret and her family is unknown.

"Prigg vs. Pennsylvania (1842). When the most famous female runaway slave, Harriet Tubman, crossed the line from Maryland to Pennsylvania, in 1849, she felt as if she had almost been born again! As she later remembered it: 'When I found I had crossed the line, I looked at my hands to see if I was the same person. There was such a glory over everything; the sun came like gold through the trees, and over the fields, and I felt like I was in Heaven.'

"Prigg vs. Pennsylvania is the story of an earlier Maryland runaway, Margaret Morgan, of a Pennsylvania lawyer who told the Supreme Court that the policy concerning escaped slaves threatened the foundations of the Republic, and of the curious results of the inconsistencies expressed by the court.

"In 1814, a farmer, John Ashmore, greatly enlarged his property in northern Harford County, Maryland. He soon became a slave-owning planter, mixing with the older slave owners of the area including the Prigg, Lewis and Forwood families. His property included a water-driven grain mill associated with the village of Mill Green. In 1828 he gave most of his property to his daughter and son-in-law, Susanna and Nathan Bemis, and died soon after.

"Ashmore's slaves, including the young female Margaret, belonged to his widow, Margaret Ashmore, but the slave Margaret married a free black, Jerry Morgan, and considered herself free. She was listed as free in the federal census of 1830 although she had no papers of manumission. Changes in agricultural methods in northern Maryland in the late 1820s led to a period when large numbers of slaves were no longer productively useful. Eliminating their upkeep was a saving; selling them out of the State was not yet practical. Some farmers simply told their slaves to depart, and it is likely the Ashmore-Bemis farm followed that course.

"In 1832, the Morgans left, and established themselves in York, Pennsylvania, where their second child was born. In 1837, Margaret Ashmore authorized Nathan Bemis and three other slave owners of northern Harford County, Jacob Forwood, Stephen Lewis and Edward Prigg, to bring back Margaret and her children.

"The Constitution contained a section authorizing recapture of escaped slaves and indentures servants, but failed to say how they should be claimed and delivered: 'No person held to Service or Labour in one State, under the Laws thereof, escaping into another, shall, in Consequence of any Law or Regulation therein, be discharged from such Service or Labour, but shall be delivered up on Claim of the Party to whom such Service or Labour may be due."

"Did other statements in the Constitution, such as the criminal extradition clause in Article IV, mean that the state to which a slave fled had an obligation to return the slave to the owner? No one was certain.

"In 1793, Congress had passed the first Fugitive Slave Act, which was in force until superceded the second Fugitive Slave Act, in 1850, a direct result of the furor that arose from Margaret Morgan's case. The 1793 act stated that slave masters or their agents could seize runaways in other states, bring them before any federal or state court in the state where seizure occurred, and – upon proving the slaves; identity by documents or sworn statements – take them back under the court's authority. Beginning in 1824, however, several northern states passed statutes outwardly intended to implement the Act of 1793, but deliberately creating requirements that made slave recovery complicated. The complications were meant to prevent legally free blacks from being kidnapped into slavery. There were known as 'personal liberty laws.' In view of the difficulties of identifying individual blacks, their minimum education, the eclipsed rights of free blacks and the imprecise legal standards, it was no wonder the free blacks were being kidnapped.

"Pennsylvania's personal liberty law, passed in 1826, was a strange compromise. Pennsylvania had established 'gradual emancipation' in 1780, so that the only slaves in Pennsylvania were that lingering group that had been enslaved before 1780. Only 64 remained in 1840; all had passed away by 1850. In 1820, the General Assembly moved toward a personal liberty law by passing a statute providing that anyone removing free blacks from the state was kidnapping. In 1826, this law was supplemented to provide that slave owners (or their agents) could seize blacks they were certain were their slaves under warrants from any Pennsylvania magistrate, whether a judge, J. P., or alderman. But the apprehending person had to complete very exacting forms before a Pennsylvania warrant could be issued, requirements far more complicated than those of the federal Fugitive Slave Act. If owners or agents chose to try to recover a slave under the federal act, they were not allowed to apply to the lower Pennsylvania magistrates, the J. P.s and alderman. It was clear that the 1826 law made it much more difficult for slave owners to real runaway slaves in Pennsylvania. It was truly a personal liberty law.

"In the late 1830 anti-black sentiment, along with other reactionary influences, swelled in Pennsylvania. A new state constitution in 1837 disenfranchised free blacks, and the burning of a new center for reform activities, Philadelphia Hall, in 1838, was another example of rising public intolerance. Pennsylvanians had divided feelings concerning those who came to recapture runaway slaves. There were many abolitionists, and there were others, who though callous toward slavery, objected to the violence that slave hunting aroused. Although the most famous incidence of violence, the Christiana Riot in Lancaster County, in 1851, was many years away, the areas adjacent to Maryland had often been troubled. In 1821, a Baltimore slave owner and his assistant were killed in Pennsylvania while trying to recover a slave. In 1825, a man transporting two slaves back to Maryland was attacked in York and his carriage was cut to pieces. In York, opposition to slavery came both from a group of whites and from a community of free blacks which had arrived there in 1828 as migrants from Virginia. The expression 'Underground Railroad' may have originated in York. A free black entrepreneur, William C. Goodridge, arranged and financed escape routes from his home at 123 Philadelphia Street. Many slaves escaped on the thirteen railroad cars that Goodridge owned for his merchandising business, which ran back and forth between York and Philadelphia.

"When Bemis and party located Margaret in York, they obtained a magistrate's warrant and accompanied by a constable brought her and her children to a York justice of the peace, Thomas Henderson, but he refused to hear Bemis' statements identifying her as a slave. The hearing was refused on the basis of the Pennsylvania statute. We do not know whether there had been a scuffle when Margaret was seized, nor is there any information about the role of Jerry Morgan. Bemis had hoped to use sworn statements about Margaret's status, because he did not have the written documents required by the Pennsylvania law. Bemis' statements would have qualified under the federal Fugitive Slave Act, but there was no federal court available. Therefore, the party took the mother and children back to Harford County without legal authorization. Pennsylvania indicted the slave hunters for kidnapping and began the extradition process. Meanwhile, Bemis sold Margaret. Governor Thomas Veazey and his advisers took the initiative and decided to work toward a decision by the Supreme Court, rather than trying to placate both sides, having the prosecution dropped, and waiting until another crisis developed over runaways. Thoroughly frightened, Bemis followed orders and bought Margaret back. From the start Maryland admitted that the children should not have been involved.

"Personal communications between the governors and high officials of both states took place, and special legislation was passed in Harrisburg allowing Bemis to appear before a York County grand jury. In the end, Bemis, Forwood and Lewis were dropped from the proceedings which reached the Supreme Court, so that technically Edward Prigg was the only defendant in the final case. In order to test Pennsylvania's position, the sheriff of Harford County was sent to York to bring back a black who was wanted in Maryland. The same scenario was repeated. The sheriff received a magistrate's warrant, but a York J. P. refused him a hearing when he appeared with his prisoner. Threatened with a kidnapping charge, the sheriff gave up and went home.

"After four and a half years of special handling and delays, the Supreme Court heard the case. In January 1842, the Supreme Court determined that the Pennsylvania law was an interference with the slave recovery provisions of the Constitution. In the process it also upheld the federal Fugitive Slave Act. The lawyers for Pennsylvania, Attorney General Ovid F. Johnson, and the York County deputy attorney general, Thomas C. Hambly, delivered long arguments in a vain effort to defend the Pennsylvania statute. Hambly won a moral victory, however, because he was able to work into his argument strong comments about the true national ferment over slavery. He broke through the bounds of professional politeness that usually inhibited lawyers. In fact, his superior, Johnson, had to apologize for Hambly's having lectured to the nation's highest jurists. Hambly, who had a private practice in addition to his work as a deputy to the state's attorney general, was York's leader of legal opposition to slavery. Although personally ambitious and interested mostly in wealthy clients, Hambly's abolitionist bias arose from sincere humanitarian beliefs.

"The opinion of the Supreme Court was written by a famous judge and profound legal theorist, Joseph Story. Seldom, however, has a decision been so misunderstood. Intended to clarify a problem that had caused trouble for many years, this decision ironically gave rise to another period of doubt.

"After holding that the statute was unconstitutional, Story elaborated, saying that the power to legislate how the recovery of escaped slaves could take place lay exclusively with Congress. This went beyond the legal issues presented by Margaret Morgan's kidnapping. It could have been construed as Story's personal view, not as a binding interpretation of the Constitution. In fact, six of the other judges wrote opinions which, although agreeing with Story that the Pennsylvania statute was unconstitutional, took differing views about the rights of states to regulate activities of slave hunters. In general, the judges from the South felt that sates could pass laws assisting the recovery parties, as long as these laws were not disguised personal liberty laws. But some of the judges appointed from northern state opposed any form of state law on the subject, coming close to Story's position.

"Story also said that states could pass laws withholding the services of some of their magistrates, even though this seemed almost to contradict his opinion that they could not specify a process for recovering runaways. To add to the confusion, he said that although owners had a constitutional right to seize runaway slaves, if violence resulted the states were entitled to take legal action against the slave hunters to preserve peace within their borders. None of his fellow judges backed him on these points.

"Because of the inconsistencies in Story's opinion and in those of the concurring judges, six northern states passed new personal liberty laws before 1850. All these interfered in some manner with the return of runaway slaves, as well as protecting free blacks from being falsely identified as slaves. Pennsylvania lawyers stubbornly took the view that the law of 1825 was only partially unconstitutional. In 1847 the General Assembly passed a new personal liberty law which, like the 1826 law, included penalties against kidnapping, but changed the wording by adding the adjective 'free' before all references to 'negro and mulatto.' It prohibited all Pennsylvania magistrates and judges from presiding at hearings under the federal Fugitive Slave Act. Technically, these changes conformed to the Prigg case decision, but their impact defied it because the question of whether a seized black was free or not was what the hearings under the 1826 Act had been all about. Blacks who had been seized and whose free status was questionable would still, in any law-abiding Pennsylvania community, be brought before Pennsylvania authorities if they claimed that they were free, providing it was done before they were made to appear before federal courts. Of course, there were very few federal courts available. The 1847 law also forbid the use of Pennsylvania's jails to hold blacks before they had hearings, and, for the first time, allowed blacks to testify in their own defense. Thus, summary retention of blacks suspected of being runaways, while awaiting a federal court hearing, was unlikely to occur.

"It was not a lasting solution, however. The new personal liberty laws increased animosities to the point where a national compromise had to be agreed to in Congress, part of which was a new federal Fugitive Slave Law. This was the Compromise of 1850. For the first time federal marshals were authorized to enforce the law. Now the nation was on a collision course toward secession.

"How should history judge the Prigg case? It seems likely that if the court's opinion had been more straightforward the stages leading to the Civil War would have taken some other patters. But the court's understanding of its role prevented it from speaking directly to points of national political and moral sentiment. Thus, the Supreme Court could not have been expected to have arrived at just such a confusing position." (Ref: Undated typescript filed in the Archives of the Historical Society of Harford County, compiler not stated; and, some information found in their Court Records Documents 103.15.1 and 114.12.4; "Harford had Little Known Role in Origins of Civil War – Supreme Court Case on Margaret Morgan Put U.S. on Path to Conflict," by Allan Vought, *The Aegis*, 21 Feb 2018, contained information provided by local African American researchers and lecturers Iris L. Barnes and Jacob Bensen from their recent "Sacrificing Margaret Morgan" lecture)

Mulatto Andrew. "$200 Reward – Ran away from Harford County, about the middle of January [1858], my mulatto man Andrew, 28 years old, about 6 feet high, square built, remarkably large hands and feet, hair very bushy when combed out, but he generally wears it in plaits [pleats or braids]; has little to say when spoken to; had on when he left a short country-made drab Coat and drab Pantaloons; had also a new gray Coat and other clothing. It is thought he is loitering about this city [Baltimore] or Harford. The above reward will be paid if taken and secured in any jail in the State so that I get him again. W. J. Polk, 78 McCulloch street." (Ref: *Baltimore Sun*, 11 Mar 1858)

Mulatto George. "Ran away, from the Subscriber, living in Harford County, on Saturday the 7th Instant [June 1783], a Mulatto Man named George, about 32 Years of Age, 5 feet 6 Inches high; had on, when he went away, an old white Fustian Coat, an old brown Cloth Jacket, --?-- Cloth Breeches, a Pair of old blue ribb'd Stockings, a Pair of Shoes with Buckles, a white linen Shirt, and a Felt Hat, with a Buckle and Ribband [ribbon] around the Crown – Whoever takes up the said Fellow, and brings him home, shall have, if taken within 16 Miles of home, *Four Dollars*; if 20 miles, *Six Dollars*; if 30 Miles, *Eight Dollars*; and if out of the State, *Ten Dollars*, paid by William Worthington. N. B. He plays the violin. June 26, 1783." (Ref: *Maryland Journal and Baltimore Advertiser*, 1 Jul 1783)

June 26, 1783

Ran away, from the Subſcriber, living in Harford County, on Saturday the 7th Inſtant, a *Mulatto Man* named GEORGE, about 32 Years of Age, 5 Feet 6 Inches high; Had on, when he went away, an old white Fuſtian Coat, an old brown Cloth Jacket, blue Cloth Breeches, a Pair of old blue ribb'd Stockings, a Pair of Shoes with Buckles, a white Linen Shirt, and a Felt Hat, with a Buckle and Ribband around the Crown —— Whoever takes up the ſaid Fellow, and brings him home, ſhall have, if taken within 16 Miles of home, *Four Dollars*; if 20 Miles, *Six Dollars*; if 30 Miles, *Eight Dollars*; and if out of the State, *Ten Dollars*, paid by

WILLIAM WORTHINGTON.

N. B. He plays on the violin.

Mulatto Jack. "May 1, 1776. Six Dollars Reward. – Run away from the subscriber, living in Harford County, Maryland, a Mulattoe Slave, named Jack, well set, is about 5 feet 6 inches high, very white for one of his kind, speaks good English, is a very great rogue. The said Slave was taken up and put in Lancaster [PA] goal [jail] on the first of July 1775, and made his escape from William Whiteford coming home. The said fellow said he had been in New York goal as a runaway, but by reason of my advertisement not going there, was let out, and says he had been on board the kingships of war, and that he was at the West Indies; it is thought he will endeavour to get to the ministerial army; he had changed his name to Jacob Kelly. Any person who takes up said Slave is requested to deal severely with him, and if taken up by this advertisement, is desired to put him in Dunlap paper. Whoever takes up said Slave shall have the above reward paid by Hugh Whiteford. N.B. The subscriber requests this advertisement may be carefully kept and taken notice of for several years." (Ref: *The Pennsylvania Gazette*, 24 Jul 1776)

Mulatto Joe. "Baltimore, May 30, 1780. Fifty Pounds Reward. Ran away from the subscriber plantation, about nine miles from this town, a mulatto fellow named Joe. He is very likely and stout made, 25 years old, about 5 feet 10 inches high, has a scar on one of his wrists, and walks very erect. – Had on and took with him, a white cloth surtout coat, an old blue regimental coat, faced with red, and the sleeves, from the elbows, mended with white cloth, white cloth waistcoat, lined with blue linsey woolsey, a pair of linen corded breeches, one pair of linen and one paid of blue worsted overalls, one pair of tow linen trowsers, three shirts, a black stock, pair of blue ribbed worsted stockings, a new wool hat, with a brass button to it, and pair of French leather shoes, with brass buckles. He has much the appearance of having been in the army, where he was some time a waggoner. He is very plausible in speech, and will probably attempt to pass as a free man, by the name Joseph Hanson. It is likely he may attempt to pass towards Bush

Town [in Harford, County], near where his mother lives. – Whoever takes up the said runaway, and secures or brings him to my plantation, William Andrew, overseer, or to me in this town, shall receive the above reward, and all reasonable charges. Matthew Ridley." (Ref: *The Pennsylvania Gazette*, 7 Jun 1780)

Mulatto Lewis. "One Dollar Reward. Ran away from the subscriber, from on board the Schooner William, now lying at McElderry's Wharf, Baltimore, a dark Mulatto Boy, named Lewis, about five feet four or five inches high, had on when he went away a pair of kersey trowsers and roundabout jacket, made out of a drab colored coat. Masters of vessels and others are forbid harboring him at their peril, as they will be dealt with as the rigor of the law will direct. Whoever will take up said boy and secure him in Baltimore goal [jail] shall receive the above reward. James Taylor, Abington [Abingdon], Harford County." (Ref: *Maryland Journal and Baltimore Advertiser*, 1 Apr 1809)

Mulatto Rachel. "Six Dollars Reward. Ran Away, from the subscriber, about two Years ago, a remarkably fair Mulatto Woman Slave, named Rachel; she is 45 Years of Age, very spare made, wears long Hair; had a Scar on her Neck, caused by a Burn. – Whoever secures the said Mulatto Slave, shall have the above Reward, and reasonable Charges, if brought home, paid by Samuel Lee. Harford County, April 14, 1790." (Ref: *Maryland Journal and Baltimore Advertiser*, 20 Apr 1790)

Myers, John. "Arrival from Harford Co. [to Philadelphia], 1857. John had fled from under the yoke of Dr. Joshua R. Nelson. Until within two years of 'Jack's' flight, the doctor 'had been a very fine man,' with whom Jack found no fault.

But suddenly his mode of treatment changed; he became very severe. Nothing that Jack could do met the approval of the doctor. Jack was constantly looked upon with suspicion.

"The very day that Jack fled, four men approached him (the doctor one of them), with line in hand; that sign was well understood, and Jack resolved that they should not get within tying distance of him. 'I dodged them,' said Jack. Never afterwards was Jack seen in that part of the County, at least as long as a fetter remained.

"The day that he 'dodged' he also took the Underground Rail Road, and although ignorant of letters, he battled his way out of Maryland, and succeeded in reaching Pennsylvania and the Committee. He was obliged to leave four children behind – John, Abraham, Jane and Ellen.

"Jack's wife had been freed and had come to Philadelphia two years in advance of him. His master evidently supposed that Jack would be mean enough to wish to see his wife, even in a free State, and that no slave, with such an unnatural desire, could be tolerated or trusted, that the sooner such 'articles' were turned into cash the better. This in substance, was the way Jack accounted for the sudden change which had come over his master. In defense of his course, Jack referred to the treatment which he had received while in servitude under his old master, in something like the following words: 'I served under my young master's father, thirty-five years, and from him received kind treatment. I was his head man on the place, and had everything to look after." (Ref: *The Underground Railroad*, by William Still, 1871, repr. 1970, p. 452)

Myres, Independent. 1858. "$200 Reward. – Ran Away from the subscriber, Two Negro Men, one about thirty years of age, about five feet five inches high, somewhat spotted on his arms and body, and named Independent Myres. The other [name was not reported] is about twenty years of age, five feet ten inches, black, and stutters considerable in conversation. It is supposed that they are somewhere in the city of Baltimore as one of them formerly lived there, and has relatives in the place. The above reward will be given to any person or persons who will bring them to me or secure them in jail so that I can get them. James Carlin, Shawsville P. O., Harford County, Md." (Ref: *Baltimore Sun*, 11 Nov 1858)

Negro Adam. Advertisement dated 6 Mar 1777: "Thirty Dollars Reward. Ran away on the 25th day of September, 1776, a Negro man named Adam, about 24 years of age, very black, tall and slender, a cunning artful fellow, stammers a little when frightened, he formerly belonged to William Presbury, bricklayer, and was brought up to the bricklayer business; he ran away about 18 months ago, and got to Grubb's Iron works, above Lancaster, in Pennsylvania; Had on when he went away, an old felt hat, old shoes, tow linen short and trousers, whitish coloured country cloth jacket much worn, has had the small pox about 18 months ago, and has a remarkable large foot. Whoever takes up and secures said Negro, so as his master may have hi m again, shall have, if taken in the County, Five Pounds; if taken out of the County and in the State of Maryland, Seven Pounds Ten Shillings; and if out of the State the above reward, and reasonable charges, if brought home, from Peter Bond, living in Harford County, about six miles from Joppa." (Ref: *Maryland Journal and Baltimore Advertiser*, 11 Mar 1777)

March 6, 1777.

THIRTY DOLLARS Reward.

RAN away on the 25th day of September, 1776, a Negro man named ADAM, about 34 years of age, very black, tall and ſlender, a cunning artful fellow, ſtammers a little when frightened, he formerly belonged to William Preſbury, bricklayer, and was brought up to the bricklaying buſineſs; he ran away about 18 months ago, and got to Grubb's Iron Works, above Lancaſter, in Pennſylvania: Had on when he went away, an old felt hat, old ſhoes, tow linen ſhirt and trowſers, whitiſh coloured country cloth jacket much worn, has had the ſmall pox about 18 months ago, and has a remarkable large foot. Whoever takes up and ſecures ſaid Negro, ſo as his maſter may have him again, ſhall have, if taken in the county, Five Pounds; if taken out of the county and in the State of Maryland, Seven Pounds Ten Shillings; and if out of the State the above reward, and reaſonable charges, if brought home, from PETER BOND, living in Harford county, about ſix miles from Joppa.

Negro Alex. 1861. "Runaway Negroes. Four negro men, George, Charles, Santy and Alex, belonging to Thomas A., Hays, Esq., of this place [Bel Air], left home on Sunday morning last [2 Jun 1861], to go fishing, as they said, but the last heard of them they had taken the cars at Perryville, opposite Havre-de-Grace, for Philadelphia. The negro man who conveyed them across the river at Havre-de-Grace has been arrested and is now in Bel Air jail. – They applied at the ticket office, we learn, on Sunday for tickets to Philadelphia, but being refused them, they loitered about Perryville for some time, when by some means they got on the train for Philadelphia and went off. The Railroad Company being informed of the facts, immediately telegraphed the intelligence to that place.

"The mule belonging to their master and the horse and carriage which they hired from citizens of Bel Air, by which to make their escape, they left in Havre-de-Grace.

"Four hundred dollars reward is offered for the arrest of the four men and the delivery of the property which they took with them.

"Mr. Hays has also offered two hundred dollars for the arrest of a negro man names Sam, who ran away one year ago, and fifty dollars for another, (old negro), named Santy, who went away about three weeks ago." (Ref: *National American*, 7 Jun 1861)

Negro Basil. "Was committed to the Gaol of Baltimore County on the 9th day of April, 1830, by Joseph Benson, Esq., a Justice of the Peace for the City of Baltimore – as a runaway, a negro Man, who calls himself Joseph alias Basil and says he belongs to Doctor Willian Conoway [actually William D. Conway] of Harford County; said negro is five feet four inches high and about thirty years of age; had on when committed, a Linsey Woolsey Roundabout and Pantaloons, Green Waistcoat, Cotton Shirt, Coarse Shoes, Stockings and old Fur Cap. The owner of the above-described negro man is requested to come forward, prove property, pay charges and take him away; otherwise, he will be discharged according to law. David W. Hudson, Warden of Baltimore County Jail." (Ref: *Baltimore Gazette and Daily Advertiser*, 16 Apr 1830)

Negro Bateman. 1791. "Ran away from the Northampton Furnace in Baltimore County on Saturday night the twenty-third Inst. A negro man named Bateman, about twenty-one years of age, about six feet high, lusty & well made, rather of a yellow complexion, has had a cut on one of his knees & the scar is remarkably fresh, he is a well looking negroe, had on when he went away a dark olive coloured cloth coat with large yellow buttons, full trim'd. striped cassimere vest blue & white, fustian overalls of an olive colour, new hat, holland shirt & good shoes & buckles, he formerly belonged to Maulden Amos in Harford County, whoever takes him up & brings home said negro if Ten miles from home shall receive Thirty Shillings, if Twenty miles forty five Shillings, if Thirty miles Three Pounds, if Sixty miles Four Pounds, if one hundred miles Five Pounds, & if one hundred & fifty miles the above reward & reasonable charges if brought home, paid by Charles Ridgely. 26th April 1791." (Copy courtesy of James E. Chrismer, of Bel Air, MD, 2019)

Negro Ben. "Thirty Dollars Reward. Ran away from the subscriber, living in Hartford *(sic)* County, in the state of Maryland, on the 4th of June last [1778], a negro man named Ben, a stout well set fellow, about five feet seven or eight inches high, thirty eight years of age, very black, his two fore teeth remarkable far from each other; he is a sensible artful fellow – His clothing is, a good plain country cloth coat, leather breeches, or tow linen trowsers, a half warn castor hat, and good shoes and buckles: He has sundry other cloths, which perhaps he may change for regimentals, and it is supposed, by what he communicated to some of his companions, he will endeavour to got *(sic)* to the enemy. Whoever takes up said Negro and secures him, so that his master may get him again, shall have Fifteen Dollars, or if brought home the above reward and reasonable charges. William Hopkins, Junior." (Ref: *The Pennsylvania Packet*, 4 Jul 1778)

Negro Ben. [document was partially torn off] "... Shadrick Johnson, and I suppose had a pass, which very likely Leander has got from him. Ben is about 20 years of age, of a yellowish complexion, and about 5 feet 9 or 10 inches high; his clothing is not know *(sic)* as he has lately got a new suit. Both of the above Negros have been brought up to farming and understand it well. The above reward will be given for the above runaways, if brought home or secured in any jail so this subscriber may get them again, or one Hundred Dollars for either of them. William R. Brooke, George Walker. 30th May 1817." (Historical Society of Harford County Archives File "Slavery – Runaways")

Negro Bob. "Six Pounds (hard money) Reward. Harford County, October 5, 1782. Ran away, from Spesutie-Island, a Negro Fellow named Bob, about 5 feet 5 inches high, well set, until he had his thigh broke, which makes him go lame, as one leg and thigh are shorted than the other; has a down cast guilty look, affects to talk very politely, drinks, lies, and plays on the fiddle. Whoever delivers the said Negro to either of the subscribers, if taken out of the County, the above Reward, and if in the County, Three Pounds Specie; and if secured in gaol, out of the County, so that his master gets him again, Three Pounds Specie. Samuel Hughes, William Hall." (Ref: *Maryland Journal and Baltimore Advertiser*, 8 Oct 1782)

SIX POUNDS (hard money) REWARD.

Harford County, October 5 1782.

RAN away, from Spefutie-Iſland, *a Negro Fellow named BOB*, about 5 feet 5 inches high, well-ſet, until he had his thigh broke, which makes him go lame, as one leg and thigh are ſhorter than the other; has a down-caſt guilty look, affects to talk very politely, drinks, lies, and plays on the fiddle. Whoever delivers the ſaid Negro to either of the ſubſcribers, if taken out of the county, the above Reward, and if in the county, Three Pounds Specie; and if ſecured in gaol, out of the county, ſo that his maſter gets him again, Three Pounds Specie.

SAMUEL HUGHES,
WILLIAM HALL.

Negro Bob. "One Hundred Dollars Reward. Ran away from the subscriber, on the night of the 2nd inst. [April 1840], a negro boy, named Bob, about 21 or 22 years old, 5 feet 7 or 8 inches tall, dark complexion, low narrow forehead; has lost two of his upper front teeth, and has a scar in one of his eyebrows. Had on roundabout and pantaloons of country made cloth; but carried with him a frock coat, black vest, and black ribbed cassimere pantaloons, with other clothing, and supposed to be supplied with money. The above reward will be paid on his delivery to the subscriber in Bel-Air, or his being secured in jail, so that I get him. Henry Dorsey, of Edw'd. Bel-Air, April 3rd, 1840." (Ref: *Baltimore Sun*, 9 Apr 1840)

Negro Boston. "Forty Dollars Reward. Ran Away, from the subscriber, on Monday the 26th of July, a Negro Man named Boston (it is probable he may change his Name) – He is about 5 Feet 7 or 8 Inches high, stout made, dark Complexion, down Look, and when spoken sharply to stammers; had on, and took with him, a Felt Hat, short round brown Jacket with sleeves, Two Tow-Linen Shirts and Trousers, and old Shoes, his other Clothes, if any, unknown. It is supposed he had directed his Course towards Philadelphia. Whoever takes up the said Negro, and delivers him to the Subscriber, living on Swan-Creek, Harford County, shall receive, if taken 20 Miles from Home, Thirty Shillings; if 40 Miles, Three Pounds; if 50 Miles, Five Pounds; if 60 miles, Seven Pounds; and if 100 Miles and upwards, the above Reward, with reasonable Charges, paid by Alexander Lawson Smith. Harford County, August 2, 1790." (Ref: *Maryland Journal and Baltimore Advertiser*, 6 Aug 1790)

Negro Bowie. "A Runaway Negro. Ran Away, from the subscriber, living in Fork of Gunpowder, near Meredith's Ford, Negro Bowie, a likely young fellow, about 5 feet 7 or 8 inches high, 23 years of age, or thereabouts. – He had a down look, and his tongue is so glib that he is nicknamed Lawyer – he is well cloathed, having a jacket and breeches of white kersey, new osnaburg shirt, good yarn stockings, and his shoes plated at the toes – one of his shoes has been cut with an axe from the sole upwards, near where the quarter and vamp join, and has been sewed up. Whoever will secure the said Negro in any gaol, or will deliver him to me, shall have Six Dollars reward, if he is within five miles of home, and Five Pounds, if at the distance of sixteen miles. George Fitzhugh. January 8, 1785." (Ref: *Maryland Journal and Baltimore Advertiser*, 1 Feb 1785)

A RUNAWAY NEGRO.

RAN AWAY, from the ſubſcriber, living in the Fork of Gunpowder, near Meredith's Ford, Negro BOWIE, a likely young fellow, about 5 feet 7 or 8 inches high, 23 years of age, or thereabouts.---He has a down look, and his tongue is ſo glib that he is nicknamed *Lawyer*---he is well cloathed, having a jacket and breeches of white kerſey, new oſnaburg ſhirt, good yarn ſtockings, and his ſhoes plated at the tees---one of his ſhoes has been cut with an axe from the ſole upwards, near where the quarter and vamp join, and has been ſewed up. Whoever will ſecure the ſaid Negro in any gaol, or will deliver him to me, ſhall have SIX DOLLARS reward, if he is within five miles of home, and FIVE POUNDS, if at the diſtance of ſixteen miles.

January 8, 1785. GEORGE FITZHUGH.

Negro Caroline. In 1830 Henry Dorsey, son of Edward, of Bel Air, offered rewards for these runaway negroes: Dinah, age about 52, black; Caroline, daughter of Dinah, age about 34; three sons of Caroline: Bob, age 12, Philip, age 10, and, Joe, age 8; Charles, age about 21; Harriet, sister of Charles, age about 23. (Ref: *Independent Citizen*, 30 Sep 1830; *Newspaper Abstracts of Cecil & Harford Counties, 1822-1830*, by F. Edward Wright, 1984, p. 55)

Negro Charles. "Twenty Dollars Reward. Ran Away on the 7th day of October last [1792], from the subscriber, living in Harford County, state of Maryland, near Deer Creek, a Negroe Man, named Charles, about 25 years old, about five fee 9 or 10 inches high; has a sore on his right hand, which it is likely he will endeavour to conceal by wearing a glove; he is very black, artful and insinuating in his manners, seldom speaks without smiling; Had on and took with him when he went away, a country cloth jacket, a light blue coat, a pair of boots and shoes; but it is probable he may change his cloaths and name. Whoever takes up said fellow, so that his master may get him again, shall receive the above reward, and all reasonable charges, paid by Barnard Preston, senior, Harford County, January 5, 1793." (Ref: *The Pennsylvania Gazette*, 16 Jan 1793)

Negro Charles. "One Hundred Dollars Reward. Left my Farm in Harford County, on Saturday, the 11th day of April [1857], Negro man Charles, about 25 years old, five feet seven or eight inches high, and very black. The most notable mark about him is, four of his toes are off one of his feet. He is still and slow in his manners. I will give the above reward if he is taken out of the State, or fifty dollars if taken in the State. In either case he must be brought home to me, or secured so that I may get him. William L. Wheeler." (Ref: *Harford Democrat*, 1 May 1857)

One Hundred Dollars Reward.

Left my Farm in Harford county, on Saturday, the 11th day of April, NEGRO MAN CHARLES, about 25 years old, five feet seven or eight inches high, and very black. The most notable mark about him is, four of his toes are off one of his feet. He is still and slow in his manners. I will give the above reward if he is taken out of the State, or fifty dollars if taken in the State. In either case he must be brought home to me, or secured so that I may get him.

ap24 WILLIAM L. WHEELER.

Negro Charles. “1822. Commonwealth vs. Jesse Cutler and Joseph Stubbs} Habeas Corpus for the body of Negro Boy named Charles. 'By act of the Assembly of 1785.' Lancaster County, ss. The Commonwealth of Pennsylvania, to Jesse Cutler & Joseph Stubbs, Greetings: You are hereby commanded, that the body of Negro Boy named Charles under your or one of your custody detained, as it is said, together with the day and cause of his being taken and detained, by whatsoever name the said Negro Boy named Charles shall be charged in the same, you have, under safe and secure conduct, before the honorable Samuel Dale, Esquire, one of the Judges of the Court of Common Pleas of Lancaster County at his office in the City of Lancaster on Tuesday the 23rd of April instant [1822] at ten o'clock in the fore noon; to do and receive all those things which the said Judge shall then and there consider of in this particular. Witness the honorable Walter Franklin, Esquire, President of the Court of Common Pleas of said County, at Lancaster, the Eighteenth day of April in the year of our Lord, one thousand eight hundred and twenty-two. T. Muhlenberg,

Prot(?). Allowed by Samuel Dale." (Historical Society of Harford County, Archives Document)

Negro Charles. In 1830 Henry Dorsey, son of Edward, of Bel Air, offered rewards for these runaway negroes: Dinah, age about 52, black; Caroline, daughter of Dinah, age about 34; three sons of Caroline: Bob, age 12, Philip, age 10, and, Joe, age 8; Charles, age about 21; Harriet, sister of Charles, age about 23. (Ref: *Independent Citizen*, 30 Sep 1830; *Newspaper Abstracts of Cecil & Harford Counties, 1822-1830*, by F. Edward Wright, 1984, p. 55)

Negro Charles. "Committed to jail [Bel Air], runaway negro man, Charles; he says he belongs to Sheppard C. Leakin of Balt.; he is about 5 ft 5 inches, age 19-20, light complexion." (Ref: *Independent Citizen*, 19 Aug 1830; *Newspaper Abstracts of Cecil & Harford Counties, 1822-1830*, by F. Edward Wright, 1984, p. 54)

Negro Charles. "Runaway Negroes. Four negro men, George, Charles, Santy and Alex, belonging to Thomas A., Hays, Esq., of this place [Bel Air], left home on Sunday morning last [2 Jun 1861], to go fishing, as they said, but the last heard of them they had taken the cars at Perryville, opposite Havre-de-Grace, for Philadelphia. The negro man who conveyed them across the river at Havre-de-Grace has been arrested and is now in Bel Air jail. – They applied at the ticket office, we learn, on Sunday for tickets to Philadelphia, but being refused them, they loitered about Perryville for some time, when by some means they got on the train for Philadelphia and went off. The Railroad Company being informed of the facts, immediately telegraphed the intelligence to that place.

"The mule belonging to their master and the horse

and carriage which they hired from citizens of Bel Air, by which to make their escape, they left in Havre-de-Grace.

"Four hundred dollars reward is offered for the arrest of the four men and the delivery of the property which they took with them.

"Mr. Hays has also offered two hundred dollars for the arrest of a negro man names Sam, who ran away one year ago, and fifty dollars for another, (old negro), named Santy, who went away about three weeks ago." (Ref: *National American*, 7 Jun 1861)

TEN DOLLARS REWARD.

RAN away, from the ſubſcribers, the 18th day of September laſt, a NEGRO MAN named DAN, about 22 years of age, about 5 feet 10 inches high, a bold ſtout, impudent fellow, very broad between the ſhoulders, has a remarkable big under lip, ſmall legs and feet, very fond of ſtrong liquor, and ſings and ſwears much when drunk. Said Negro was bought of Archibald Beatty in Buſh-River Neck, laſt ſpring. Had on when he went away, an old beaver hat, much broken in the brim, two tow linen ſhirts and trouſers, an old white coat wanting the ſleeves, an old brown ditto. Whoever takes up ſaid Negro, ſhall have the above Reward, and reaſonable charges, if brought home paid by

MATTHEW WILEY, or
DAVID WILEY.

Harford County, Sept. 25, 1782.

Negro Dan. "Ten Dollars Reward. Ran away, from the subscribers, the 18th day of September last [1782] a Negro Man named Dan, about 22 years of age, about 5 feet 10 inches high, a bold, stout, impudent fellow, very broad between the shoulders, has a remarkable big under lip, small legs and feet, very fond of strong drink, and sings and swears much when drunk. Said Negro was bought of Archibald Beatty in Bush-River Neck, last spring. Had on, when he went away, an old beaver hat, much broken in the brim, two tow linen shirts and trousers, an old white coat wanting the sleeves, an old brown ditto [coat]. Whoever takes up said Negro, shall have the above Reward, and reasonable charges, if brought home, paid by Matthew Wiley or David Wiley. Harford County, Sept. 25, 1782." (Ref: *Maryland Journal and Baltimore Advertiser*, 29 Oct 1781)

Negro Daniel. "Four Pounds Reward. Ran away, on the 1st of June inst. [1789] two negro men, the one about 5 feet 7 or 8 inches high, about 24 years of age, can speak the German language, being bred amongst the Dutch [Deutsch, meaning German], speaks broken English, chews tobacco, which makes his teeth blackish, and called himself Peter Dawson; had on, when he went away, a felt hat, old light coloured great coat, a brown fustian straight cost, tow shirt and trowsers dyed brown, linsey jacket with broad deep blue stripes, and old shoes; was born in West Jersey, on the Delaware, and it is likely will try for that place. The other a well-made fellow, names Daniel, a shoemaker by trade, speaks good English, his cloathing not known. Whoever takes up and secures the above Negroes, so as the owner may have them again, shall have the above reward, or Two Pounds for each, and reasonable charges, paid by the subscriber, living near Haverdegrass [Havre de Grace], Harford County, State of Maryland. William Luckie." (Ref: *The Pennsylvania Gazette*, 10 Jun 1789)

Negro Davey. "Four Half Johannes Reward. Ran away, on the night of the 17th instant [April 1781], from the subscriber, living near Susquehannah lower ferry [now Havre de Grace], the two following Negro Men, viz. Davy, a tall slim black fellow, country born, about 23 years of age, upwards of 6 feet high, and lisps in his speech. – Ned, about 35 years of age, country born, about 5 feet 6 or 7 inches high, has full eyes, big legs, and one ankle larger than the other. Both of them have been used to row in the ferry-boats on Susquehannah, and are well known. Their cloathing is country-made tow shirts, and full'd cloth or linsey jacket and breeches; but as they have other clothes, and money, may change their dress. – Any person apprehending both, or either of them, and secures them, so that the subscriber gets them again, shall have, if taken within 10 miles of home, One Half Johannes; if 20 miles, Two Half Johannes; if 30 miles, Three Half Johannes; and if at a greater distance the above Reward, or in proportion for either, and reasonable charges, if brought home, paid by Samuel Thomas. April 21, 1781." (Ref: *Maryland Journal and Baltimore Advertiser*, 24 Apr 1781)

FOUR HALF JOHANNES REWARD.

RAN away, on the night of the 17th inſtant, from the ſubſcriber, living near Suſquehannah lower-ferry, the two following Negro Men, viz. DAVY, a tall ſlim black fellow, country-born, about 23 years of age, upwards of 6 feet high, and liſps in his ſpeech.—NED, about 35 years of age, country-born, about 5 feet 6 or 7 inches high, has full eyes, big legs, and one ankle larger than the other. Both of them have been uſed to row in the ferry-boats on Suſquehannah, and are well known. Their cloathing is country-made tow ſhirts, and full'd cloth or linſey jacket and breeches; but as they have other clothes, and money, may change their dreſs.——Any perſon apprehending both, or either of them, and ſecures them, ſo that the ſubſcriber gets them again, ſhall have, if taken within 10 miles of home, One Half Johannes; if 20 miles, Two Half Johannes; if 30 miles, Three Half Johannes; and if at a greater diſtance the above Reward, or in proportion for either, and reaſonable charges, if brought home, paid by SAMUEL THOMAS.

April 21, 1781.

Negro Dick. "Forty Dollars Reward. Ran away last night [3 Jan 1778] from the subscriber, living near Broad Creek, in Harford County, Maryland, two Negro men, one named Dick, about five feet six or seven inches high, down look, stoop shouldered, small limb; had on and took with him, an half worn felt hat, a tow cloth shirt, a white ditto [i. e., cloth shirt], white plush breeches, speckled stockings, old shoes, and a match coat blanket. The other named Neil, a thick well-made stout fellow, round made, talkative and speaks quick; had on a straw hat, a blue coat with a falling collar, brown thick cloth jacket laced, a tow cloth shirt, white flannel breeches, speckled stockings, and good shoes tied with thongs. Whoever takes up and secures said servants, so that their master may have them again, shall have, if 10 miles from home, ten dollars, if 20 miles twenty dollars, if 30 miles thirty dollars, if 40 miles the above reward, and reasonable charges if brought home, paid by John Barclay." (Ref: *The Pennsylvania Packet*, 21 Jan 1778)

Negro Dinah. In 1830 Henry Dorsey, son of Edward, of Bel Air, offered rewards for these runaway negroes: Dinah, age about 52, black; Caroline, daughter of Dinah, age about 34; three sons of Caroline: Bob, age 12, Philip, age 10, and, Joe, age 8; Charles, age about 21; Harriet, sister of Charles, age about 23. (Ref: *Independent Citizen*, 30 Sep 1830; *Newspaper Abstracts of Cecil & Harford Counties, 1822-1830*, by F. Edward Wright, 1984, p. 55)

Negro Doll. "Thirty Dollars Reward. Run-away from the subscriber, living near the Upper Cross Roads, in Harford County, on Tuesday, the 3rd of July [1810], a Negro Woman, about 50 years of age; grey headed; of a middle size; black complexion – she has a lively and pleasant countenance; is orderly in speech and behaviour; her teeth is nearly out before – Had with her when she went away two full suits of good new store linen, midling white, and other fine clothes: among which, is a habit of black bumbazet, and also a habit of the gayest red and white cotton callico – she also took with her out of my kitchen a large poplar chest. Her name is Doll, but will probably alter it, as well as her dress, as she had also two green baize petticoats, and a pair of shoes, part of her last winter's clothing. Whoever takes up and secures said negro woman, so that I get her again, shall receive the above reward. Tudor Chocke." (Ref: *Baltimore American*, 11 Aug 1810)

Negro Eliza. The following undated incident is from notes of "the late William W. Taylor, who was a well-known agent of the line for many years in Upper Providence Town-ship [Montgomery Co., PA]. Mr Taylor was pronounced in his hatred of the 'peculiar institution,' and ever ready to give refuge, food and transportation to those who were dispatched to his care. He was the near neighbor of Charles Corson and Thomas Hopkins, who frequently acted in concert in frustrating the designs of slave-hunters in the County. Mr. Taylor was a fearless agitator, sometimes incurring the displeasure of neighbors and acquaintances in his uncompromising denunciation of those in authority for maintaining or assenting in any way to the continuance of slavery. He was an 'Abolitionist' without qualification, an eye-witness in his boyhood days to the brutal recapture of a fugitive slave and his sale to a Southern trader at New Castle, Del. The scene made such an impression upon his mind that, to use his own words, he 'resolved that upon reaching manhood he would keep a station for runaway slaves, and he did so until the proclamation Lincoln bankrupted the business.'"

"Eliza and her son were slaves to a man named Gibbs living near Havre de Grace, Maryland. They ran off [date not given], came by way of Oxford through Chester County to F. F. Pennypacker's and on to my place [William W. Taylor]. There she wished to stay and in a short time we found we were in trouble, but we concluded to meet it. I went to Norristown, called on Thomas and Amy Bruff, stated the situation and offered to pay them to take care of her. I told them that I would find a home for her as soon as she was able to be moved, and instructed them to call on Dr. William Carson if needed and tell him I would pay all expenses. The Dr. was called on, but, as I expected, he would take nothing for his services. Her child was deformed. We took her to our place and had her for several months. Finally, the child died and was buried at the Friends' meeting-house in Providence. In the meantime, her son lived with Jacob L. Paxson. After the child died she and her son started for Canada. So, it would appear to those who stood aloof that the road of those engaged in the underground railroad was not always strewn with roses, but there was a consolation that outsiders did not understand." (Ref: *History of Montgomery County* [PA], by Theodore W. Bean, 1884, pp. 297-313, abstracted by James E. Chrismer, of Bel Air, MD, 2019)

Negro Mary. "$400 Reward. – Ran away from Farm in Harford Co., on night of September 1st [1845], a negro girl Mary, about 20 years old; color black; very short and thick; small hands and feet; flat nose, thick lips; usually combs her wool straight. Also, ran away on July 5, 1845, Negro Man Frisby, about 22 years old; color black; about 5 feet 9 or 10 inches high; upper lip thick and projecting; negro wool; knot on forehead over left eye; large nose, not very flat; walks clumsily, with his toes turned out; joints connecting big toes with feet, very large. These negroes will probably be found together. Provided they are arrested out of the State of Maryland, and I obtain possession of them, I will give the above Reward, or $200 for either, – or $100 for either if arrested in State of Maryland. A Negro Man having absconded for *(sic)* a Neighbour's Farm, at the same time, the above Girl will probably be found with him. Josiah Lee. Baltimore, Sept. 3rd, 1845." (Ref: *Baltimore American and Commercial Daily Advertiser*, 5 Sep 1845)

Negro Ephraigm. A letter dated 24 Oct 1834 from John Whisner in Philadelphia to William M. Maclaskey, in care of Dr(?) William J. McElhiney, Bel Air, Harford County. "Dear Sir, I suppose you think strange for not hearing from me sooner but the men who gave me this information where your man Tom lived was taken up soon after giving the information and I have never been able to see him since till this day and he says he will show him to me at any time I will go with him. Tom is about 20 miles from this place; there is no doubt of this information being correct as I got it from Mrs. Gallup's Mike some years since. Tom is of the description you gave and a fiddler and fond of liquor and idle. You also wish to know my lowest terms with all persons I do business for. I have one hundred and fifty dollars for taking a slave and the owner paying all expenses except the spy and the constable or one half they will bring in Maryland after all our expenses are deducted out of the sale or I will give one hundred and twenty-five dollars and I will pay all expenses of those proposals I give choice. There is also a fellow in the same neighborhood and came from your County about the same time your Tom came, he is also a yellow fellow and belongs to Mr. William Brooks of Harford County, his name at home was Ephraigm. If Mr. Brooks wishes him taken and will come or send me a power of attorney and a witness, I will take him on the same terms that I offered to take Tom for. You will please to see Mr. Brooks or let me know on the receipt of this what post office Mr. Brookes *(sic)* lives near. You will keep this information a secret at home to prevent the negro getting information as there are men in your neighborhood that would write on to the Quakers and give information. Let me hear from you soon. Yours respectfully, John Whisner, at 39 Quince Street between Ham---(?) and Locust and Spruce Sts. N. B. If you send a power of attorney be particular to have it drawn up in a proper form. J. W." On the back of the envelope: "J. G. Hoffner, No. 229 South Sixth Street, Matlock--[smudged] at Woodbury, a friend." (Ref: Historical Society of Harford County Archives Dept.)

Negro Frederic. In 1805 James Gallion, who lived at the head of Delph Creek, offered a reward for a runaway mulatto man named Frederic, about six feet high, square made, age about 23. (Ref: *Abingdon Patriot*, 1 Oct 1805)

Negro George. "40 Dollars Reward. Ran away from the subscriber living in Belle Air Harford County Md. On the 20th inst. [1809] a Negro Man named George, aged 28 years, about five feet seven or eight inches high, has a lean, crooked person, homely face, foul teeth and black skin, is slow in moving and speeking *(sic)* – Had on when he went away a half worn, black beaver hat fashionably made, spotted swans down vest, muslin shirt, two trowsers and coarse leather shoes. He was raised in Fredericksburg, Virginia and is supposed either to be making his way through Baltimore to that place, or to have gone into Chester County Pennsylvania. If taken up in Harford County and secured so that the owner get *(sic)* him, 20 dollars will be given, if out of the County the above reward, and if brought home all reasonable charges paid by Adam Clendenen. Oct 7." (Ref: *Baltimore American*, 7 Oct 1809)

Negro George. 1861. "Runaway Negroes. Four negro men, George, Charles, Santy and Alex, belonging to Thomas A., Hays, Esq., of this place [Bel Air], left home on Sunday morning last [2 Jun 1861], to go fishing, as they said, but the last heard of them they had taken the cars at Perryville, opposite Havre-de-Grace, for Philadelphia. The negro man who conveyed them across the river at Havre-de-Grace has been arrested and is now in Bel Air jail. – They applied at the ticket office, we learn, on Sunday for tickets to Philadelphia, but being refused them, they loitered about Perryville for some time, when by some means they got on the train for Philadelphia and went off. The Railroad Company being informed of the facts, immediately telegraphed the intelligence to that place.

"The mule belonging to their master and the horse and carriage which they hired from citizens of Bel Air, by which to make their escape, they left in Havre-de-Grace.

"Four hundred dollars reward is offered for the arrest of the four men and the delivery of the property which they took with them.

"Mr. Hays has also offered two hundred dollars for the arrest of a negro man names Sam, who ran away one year ago, and fifty dollars for another, (old negro), named Santy, who went away about three weeks ago." (Ref: *National American*, 7 Jun 1861)

Negro Harriet. In 1830 Henry Dorsey, son of Edward, of Bel Air, offered rewards for these runaway negroes: Dinah, age about 52, black; Caroline, daughter of Dinah, age about 34; three sons of Caroline: Bob, age 12, Philip, age 10, and, Joe, age 8; Charles, age about 21; Harriet, sister of Charles, age about 23. (Ref: *Independent Citizen*, 30 Sep 1830; *Newspaper Abstracts of Cecil & Harford Counties, 1822-1830*, by F. Edward Wright, 1984, p. 55)

Negro Harry. "West Chester, Chester County, August 2, 1790. Was committed to the gaol of this County, on the 26th of Jul last, two Negroe men, who call themselves Richard and Harry. Richard is about 5 feet 8 inches high, a stout well-made man. Harry is not quite so tall nor so thick built. They are about 30 years old each, and acknowledge themselves slaves of James Amos and Joshua Amos, of Harford County, Maryland. Their Masters are requested to come, pay charges, and take them away, otherwise they will be sold, to discharge the cost, in four weeks from this Date. Charles Dilworth, Sheriff." (Ref: *The Pennsylvania Gazette* 4 Aug 1790)

"August 14, 1790. Broke away last evening from the constable of Kennet, on their way to Westchester [West Chester] gaol, two Negroe Slaves, belonging to James and Joshua Amos, of Harford County, in the state of Maryland; the one a stout built fellow, about five feet eight or nine inches high, named Richard; the other about five feet six inches high, named Harry, both very black. Whoever apprehends and secures the above said Negroes so that they may be had, shall have Three Pounds reward for each of them, and reasonable charges, paid by the subscriber, living in Kennet township, Chester County." (Ref: *The Pennsylvania Gazette*, 6 Oct 1790)

Negro Harry. This slave of Parker Hall ran away on 26 Aug 1806. (Ref: Historical Society of Harford County, Archives File "Parker Hall – Account Book)

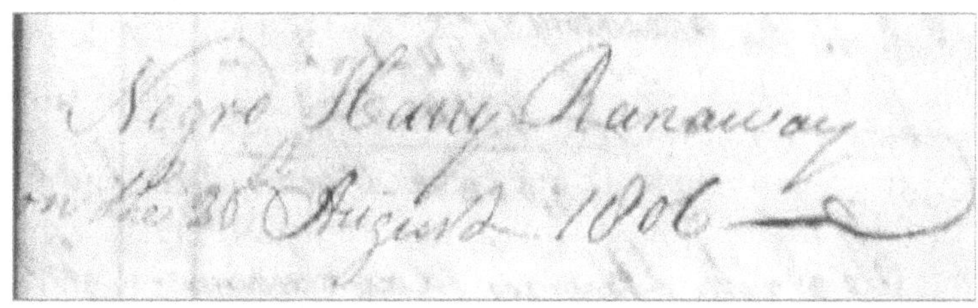
Negro Harry Ranaway
on the 26 August 1806

Negro Harry. "$100 Reward. – Ran away from the subscriber, living in Harford County, on Saturday the 6th inst. [July 1835] a Negro Man named Harry, sometimes goes by the name of 'Harry Scott.' He is a dark yellow, about 6 feet one or two inches high, and well made, supposed to have a scar on one of his hands occasioned by a burn; he is a first-rate farm hand. He had on when he went away a blue cloth coat, mazarine blue pantaloons, and took a variety of other clothing with him; he is supposed to have forged a pass. The above reward will be given if taken and secured so that I can get him again, and all reasonable charges paid if brought to the subscriber. Aquila Hall, Hall's Mill. Near Bush Town, Harford County, Md." (Ref: *Baltimore American*, 20 Jun 1835)

$100 REWARD.—Ranaway from the subscriber, living in Harford County, on Saturday the 6th inst. a Negro Man named HARRY, sometimes goes by the name of "Harry Scott." He is a dark yellow, about 6 feet one or two inches high, and well made, supposed to have a scar on one of his hands occasioned by a burn; he is a first rate farm hand. He had on when he went away a blue cloth coat, mazarine blue pantaloons, and took a variety of other clothing with him; he is supposed to have forged a pass. The above reward will be given if taken and secured so that I can get him again, and all reasonable charges paid if brought to the subscriber.

AQUILA HALL, Hall's Mill.
Near Bush Town, Harford County, Md.

Negro Henry. Letter written to Otho Scott, Esq., Bel Air, Harford County, Maryland, by A. G. Heckrotte, Allegany County, Maryland, 5 Sep 1831: "D' Sir, This moment an advertisement fell into my hands offering a reward of 750$ for 3 negroes – there is one answering the description of Henry in an adjoining County in Penna. [Pennsylvania] about 10 or 12 miles north of my residence – and is harboured by a man named Gibler [actually Kibler] who is in the habit of secreting runaway slaves, should those negroes not be yet taken if you come to my house –?-- render you any distance you may require to take them. I am myself a slave holder & live near the Penna. line on the National Road 17 miles west of Cumberland, any communication to me by mail post-paid will be properly attended to, direct to A. G. Heckrotte, Tomlinson's Post Office, Allegany County, Maryland. Respfy & Co, A. G. Heckrotte, P.S. Should this be Henry the … [illegible] … may be in the same or an adjoining neighborhood." This letter was mailed from Cumberland on 8 Sep 1831 and in the margin on the back of the envelope was written "A. G. Heckritte, Damned fool." (Ref: Historical Society of Harford County, Archives Dept.)

Negro Henry. "Runaway. Ran away from the subscriber, on Monday, the 9th of December [1861], my Negro boy, Henry, a slave for eight years. He is about 23 years old, very black, and of low stature. All persons are forewarned harboring said boy, as the law will be enforced against all such. J. J. Streett, near Clermont Mills, Harford County." (Ref: *The Southern Aegis*, 21 Dec 1861)

RUNAWAY.

RANAWAY from the subscriber, on Monday, the 9th of December, my Negro boy, HENRY, a slave for eight years. He is about 23 years old, very black, and of low stature. All persons are forewarned harboring said boy, as the law will be enforced against all such.

J. J STREETT,
near Clermont Mills,
de21 Harford County.

Negro Hyland. "One Hundred and Fifty Dollars Reward. – Ran away from the subscriber, on the 4th instant [1848], a Negro Boy, named Hyland, about 19 years old, five feet seven inches high, dark mulatto, with light blemish in one eye. Had on when he left home a drab cloth coat, gray pants and vest, and a straw hat covered with oil cloth. His clothing is stained with lime water. The above reward will be paid, if taken out of the State, or one hundred if taken in the State, and secured so that I get him again. James R. Scarff, Harford County, near Jarrettsville." (Ref: *Baltimore Sun*, 11 Nov 1848)

Negro Isaac. "100 Dollars Reward. Ran Away, on Sunday, the 27th December last [1801], a Negro Man, named Isaac, twenty-three years of age, between five feet ten inches and six feet high, yellowish black, large feet, long hands, and long round nails; had on a blue jacket, lined with flannel; coarse shoes and stockings; had not been used to work and is lazy. Whoever secures said Negro, that I may get him again, shall receive, if taken in Harford County, forty dollars; if in any other County in this State, fifty dollars; and if out of the State, the above reward paid by me. John Hall. Harford County, State of Maryland. January 8, 1802. From the Public Printing Office, by *W. C. Smyth*, High

Street, Wilmington." (Ref: Historical Society of Harford County Archives File "Slavery – Runaways")

100 Dollars Reward.

RAN AWAY, on *Sunday*, the 27th December laſt, a Negro Man, named

ISAAC,

Twenty-three years of age, between five feet ten inches and ſix feet high, yellowiſh black, large feet, long hands, and long round nails; had on a blue jacket, lined with flannel; coarſe ſhoes and ſtockings; has not been [illegible] to work, and is lazy. Whoever ſecures ſaid Negro, that I may get him again, [illegible] receive, if taken in Harford county, forty dollars; if in [illegible] county in this ſtate, ſixty dollars; and if out of the ſtate, the [illegible] Reward paid by me,

John Hall.

Harford County, ſtate of Maryland, January 8, 1802.

From the Public Printing-Office, by *W. C. Smyth*, High-ſtreet, Wilmington.

Negro Isaac. "Forty Dollars Reward. Run away from the subscriber, in King and Queen County, Virginia, about the first of November last [1783], two Virginia born Negroes, by the names of Isaac and Suck. Isaac is about 40 years of age, 6 feet high, of a yellowish complexion, with a scar over one of his eyes, and one of his arms has been broke just above the wrist. Suck is about 30 years of age, 5 feet high, very black, with one of her teeth out before, which is perceivable. They carried away different clothes with them, and a small black horse, which they stole from Virginia; their aim was Philadelphia, and I expect have gone there, as they were taken up on the main road from Baltimore to Philadelphia, in Harford County, Maryland, but made their escape. Whoever apprehends and secures the said Negroes in any goal [jail], or gives information, so that I may get them again, shall receive the above reward, paid by William Dew." (Ref: *The Pennsylvania Gazette*, 10 Dec 1783)

Negro Jack. "Six Dollars Reward. Ran Away, from the subscriber, living near Bellair, in Harford County, Maryland, on the 25th of December last [1789], a likely Negro Man, named Jack, of a yellowish complexion, round face, about 25 years of age, 5 feet 8 inches high, and well set; had on, and took with him, when he went away, a white country cloth coat and trousers, a blue cloth coat lined with red, a light white summer jacket and breeches, and other clothes not known. He is very handy at any kind of farming business. Whoever takes up said Negro, so that his master may get him again, shall receive the above reward, and reasonable charges, if brough *(sic)* home, paid by Walter Billingslea. Harford County, July 5, 1790." (Ref: *Maryland Journal and Baltimore Advertiser*, 6 Jul 1790)

Negro Jack. "The Sheriff or Jailer of Baltimore County will Please to Deliver to Mr. John Hays, a Negro man Named Jack which was Committed as the Property of Thomas R. P. Spence which I have Sold Mr. Hays or as attorney for Thos. R. P. Spence, Mr. Hays Paying the Prison and other Charges. Josiah Hubbell. Baltimore, Novr. 13Th 1816." (Ref: The Historical Society of Harford County, Archives File "Slavery – runaways")

Negro James. "Five Pounds Reward. Ran Away, from the Subscriber, living in Harford County, Gunpowder-Neck, on Sunday Morning last [May 1790], Two Negro Men, each names James. The eldest is an Ebo Negro, about 40 Years of Age, 5 Feet 4 or 5 Inches high, pitted on the Face with the Smallpox. Talks broken English, is an artful Fellow, and fond of talking: He had on, and took with him, a blue Surtout Coat, a green close-bodied Ditto [Surtout Coat], &c. &c. The other is a likely young Negro, about 21 Years of Age, 5 Feet 10 Inches high, rather slender for his Height, smooth Face, talks slow and is a great Rogue: It is uncertain what Clothes he will appear in, as he stole a Parcel the Evening before he ran away: He had on, a white Shirt, white Breeches, Fearnought Jacket, Shoes, Stockings, and a Felt Hat. Whoever takes up said Negroes, and secures them in gaol, so that I get them again, shall receive Four Dollars, for each, if taken in this State; and, if taken in any other, the above Reward, and reasonable Charges paid, if brought Home. James Weatherall. N.B. All Masters of Vessels are forewarned from carrying off said Negroes at their Peril. May 20, 1790." (Ref: *Maryland Journal and Baltimore Advertiser*, 1 Jun 1790)

Negro James. "Five Pounds Reward. Ran Away, from the Subscriber, living in Harford County, Gunpowder-Neck, on Sunday Morning last [May 1790], Two Negro Men, each names James. The eldest is an Ebo Negro, about 40 Years of Age, 5 Feet 4 or 5 Inches high, pitted on the Face with the Smallpox. Talks broken English, is an artful Fellow, and fond of talking: He had on, and took with him, a blue Surtout Coat, a green close-bodied Ditto [Surtout Coat], &c. &c. The other is a likely young Negro, about 21 Years of Age, 5 Feet 10 Inches high, rather slender for his Height, smooth Face, talks slow and is a great Rogue: It is uncertain what Clothes he will appear in, as he stole a Parcel the Evening before he ran away: He had on, a white Shirt, white Breeches, Fearnought Jacket, Shoes, Stockings, and a Felt Hat. Whoever takes up said Negroes, and secures them in gaol, so that I get them again, shall receive Four Dollars, for each, if taken in this State; and, if taken in any other, the above Reward, and reasonable Charges paid, if brought Home. James Weatherall. N.B. All Masters of Vessels are forewarned from carrying off said Negroes at their Peril. May 20, 1790." (Ref: *Maryland Journal and Baltimore Advertiser*, 1 Jun 1790)

Negro James. "Seven Hundred and Fifty Dollars Reward. – Ran away from the subscriber, living in Harford County, Md., on Sunday, 27th May last [1855], three Negro Men, named 'James,' 'Talbot,' and 'Samuel.' James is quite black, about 5 feet 9 inches high, good looking, pleasant when spoken to; 35 years old; left a free mulatto wife in the neighborhood; called himself "James Crumwell.' Talbot is a dark mulatto, 23 years old, round face, rather small eyes, 5 ft. 5 inches high, very short neck; had on a rough dark grey coat when he left; called himself 'Talbot Jones.' Samuel, a mulatto, 21 years old, front teeth broad, with a space between; delicately made, 5 ft. 7 inches high, and has a down look when spoken to, and calls himself 'Samuel Jones.' The above reward will be paid for the apprehension of the three negroes, if secured in any jail, so I can get them again, or $250 for either. William Hutchins, Taylor P. O., Harford County, Md." (Ref: *Baltimore Sun*, 4 Jul 1855)

Negro Jane. "Thomas Johnson, near Bel-Air, offers reward for colored woman named Jane, about 5 ft 8-9 inch, 31-32 years of age, broad face; she took with her a female child about 10 months old." (Ref: *Independent Citizen*, 13 Aug 1829; *Newspaper Abstracts of Cecil & Harford Counties, 1822-1830*, by F. Edward Wright, 1984, p. 41)

Negro Jem. "July 26, 1771. Ran away from the subscriber, living in the Fork of Gunpowder, Baltimore County [now

Harford County], a Negroe Man, named Jem, born in Maryland, about 5 feet 8 inches high, and 25 years of age, had on, when he went away, a white broadcloth coat, brown waistcoat, ozenbrigs trowsers, and old shoes, but it is probable will change his dress, as he was (since he ran away) concerned with several other Negroes in breaking open a store in Joppa, from which they have taken money and goods, to the amount of Forty Pounds. Whoever will apprehend the said Negroe, and have him secured in any goal, shall have a Reward of Three Pounds, and if brought home Five Pounds, and reasonable charges, paid by Samuel Young." (Ref: *The Pennsylvania Gazette*, 1 Aug 1771)

JEM; a Runaway Negro.

RAN AWAY, from Harford County, in April 1790, a NEGRO MAN, named JEM, the property of the eſtate of MATTHEW RIDLEY, Eſq; deceaſed; he is a tall ſtout Fellow, between 40 and 50 years of age, has a large flat noſe, and a remarkable wide mouth, and in ſpeaking mouths his words very much: He has a Wife and Children in Harford County, near Suſquehannah-ferry, and it is likely he is lurking thereabouts.—Whoever will take up ſaid NEGRO, and ſecure him in gaol, ſo that he is got again, ſhall have FIVE POUNDS Reward, paid by CATHERINE RIDLEY.

Baltimore, September 28, 1791.

Negro Jem. "Jem; a Runaway Negro. Ran away, from Harford County, in April 1790, a Negro Man, named Jem, the property of the estate of Matthew Ridley, Esq., deceased; he is a tall stout Fellow, between 40 and 50 years of age, has a large flat nose, and a remarkable wide mouth, and in speaking mouths his words very much: He has a Wife and Children in Harford County, near Susquehannah-ferry, and it is likely he is lurking thereabouts. – Whoever will take up said Negro, and secure him in gaol, so that he is got again, shall have Five Pounds Reward, paid by Catherine Ridley. Baltimore, September 28, 1791. (Ref: *Maryland Journal and Baltimore Advertiser*, 30 Sep 1791)

Negro Jim. "$100 Reward. Ran away from the late residence of Benjamin Buck, dec'd., in Baltimore County, on Sunday night, 29th October [1837], a negro man named Jim, belonging to the estate of said Buck – calls himself Jim Gittings. He is about 33 years of age, 5 feet 7 or 8 inches high, stout built, black, and has a pleasant countenance, no particular marks about him that are recollected. Had on when he went away, black cloth coat and fulled linzy pants, and took a quantity of other clothing, principally drab cloth.

"Jim took with him a fine black mare, about 10 years old, 14 or 15 hands high, with a star on her forehead, Fifty dollars will be given for the recovery of the negro if taken within the State, or $100 if taken without the limits of the State of Maryland, with all reasonable charges, if brought home, or lodged in jail so that I get him again, and $20 for the recovery of the mare. Henry W. Archer, Receiver. Bel Air, Nov. 9, 1837." (Ref: *The Madisonian and Harford and Baltimore Advertiser*, 7 Dec 1837)

Negro Joe. 1781. "Was delivered to my custody, a Negroe man named Joe, who served ten years with Mr. Jeremiah Strowd, in Barley *(sic)* County, Virginia, says he is now free; likewise a Negroe man, who sometimes says his name is Joe and sometimes Nero, says he lived with Mr. Isaac Webster in Hartford *(sic)* County, Maryland, near Bush-town, and with Mr. Charles Hughes, Antiatum [Antietam], Maryland, and likewise with Mr. William Jones, Maryland. The owner or owners are hereby requested to come, prove their properties, pay costs, and take them away, or they will be sold out for their costs and fees in six weeks from the date hereof. Hugh Cunningham, Goaler [Jailer]. Dec. 10, 1781. Lancaster County." (Ref: *The Pennsylvania Gazette*, 19 Dec 1781)

Negro Joe. "Six Pounds Reward. Ran Away, from the subscriber, living at Joppa, in Harford County, a Negro Man, named Joe, about 25 or 26 years of age, 5 feet 8 inches high; had on, when he went away, an oznaburg [oznabrig] shirt and trousers, light-coloured cloth jacket, and an old felt hat, but it is uncertain what clothes he will appear in, as he is a very great rogue – he is an excellent sawyer, and has been accustomed to work in a ship-yard. Whoever takes up said Negro, and secures him in gaol, so that I may get him again, shall receive, if taken in the County, Three Pounds, and if taken out of the County, the above reward, and reasonable charges if brought home, paid by Joseph Phipps. June 10, 1790." (Ref: *Maryland Journal and Baltimore Advertiser*, 22 Jun 1790)

Six Pounds Reward.

RAN AWAY, from the ſubſcriber, living at Joppa, in Harford County, a NEGRO MAN, named JOE, about 25 or 26 years of age, 5 feet 8 inches high; had on, when he went away, an oznaburg ſhirt and trouſers, light-coloured cloth jacket, and an old felt hat, but it is uncertain what clothes he will appear in, as he is a very great rogue—he is an excellent ſawyer, and has been accuſtomed to work in a ſhip-yard. Whoever takes up ſaid NEGRO, and ſecures him in gaol, ſo that I may get him again, ſhall receive, if taken in the county, THREE POUNDS, and, if taken out of the county, the above reward, and reaſonable charges, if brought home, paid by JOSEPH PHIPPS.

June 10, 1790.

Negro Joe. "Twenty Dollars Reward. Ran-Away from the subscriber, living on Specuia [Spesutia] Island, Harford

County, state of Maryland, on Monday the 1st of August, 1808, a negro boy named Joe, between 18 or 19 years old, about five feet six or eight inches high, full faced, flat nose, has considerable white in his eyes and a speck in the white of one, has an uncommon ugly walk, talks thick, and stammers when spoken to; had on a tow linen shirt and trousers, but likely to have changed his dress, having taken with him a blue jacket and two waistcoats and a Madras handkerchief. He was seen on the road going toward Baltimore, at which place his father lives. He will no doubt change his name and pass for a free man. The friends of humanity will confer a favor by apprehending the said boy, as he is manumitted, and not a slave for life. I will give the above reward for securing him in jail, so that I get him again, Gilbert Gallup. N. B. I forewarn all persons from harboring or employing the said boy." (Ref: *Baltimore American*, 20 Aug 1808)

Negro Joe. In 1830 Henry Dorsey, son of Edward, of Bel Air, offered rewards for these runaway negroes: Dinah, age about 52, black; Caroline, daughter of Dinah, age about 34; three sons of Caroline: Bob, age 12, Philip, age 10, and, Joe, age 8; Charles, age about 21; Harriet, sister of Charles, age about 23. (Ref: *Independent Citizen*, 30 Sep 1830; *Newspaper Abstracts of Cecil & Harford Counties, 1822-1830*, by F. Edward Wright, 1984, p. 55)

Negro Joseph. "Was committed to the Gaol of Baltimore County on the 9th day of April, 1830, by Joseph Benson, Esq., a Justice of the Peace for the City of Baltimore – as a runaway, a negro Man, who calls himself Joseph alias Basil and says he belongs to Doctor Willian Conoway [actually William D. Conway] of Harford County; said negro is five feet four inches high and about thirty years of age; had on when committed, a Linsey Woolsey Roundabout and Pantaloons, Green Waistcoat, Cotton Shirt, Coarse Shoes, Stockings and old Fur Cap. The owner of the above-described negro man is requested to come forward, prove property, pay charges and take him away; otherwise, he will be discharged according to law. David W. Hudson, Warden of Baltimore County Jail." (Ref: *Baltimore Gazette and Daily Advertiser*, 16 Apr 1830)

Negro Julia or Julian. 1829. "Teresa Wheeler offers reward for negro woman named Julia or Julian, age 19, 5 ft 5-6 inch, proportionally large, formerly property of Clement Green, late of Harford County, dec'd.; she has relations in Pennsylvania." (Ref: *Independent Citizen*, 13 Aug 1829; *Newspaper Abstracts of Cecil & Harford Counties, 1822-1830*, by F. Edward Wright, 1984, p. 41)

Negro Lawyer. "A Runaway Negro. Ran Away, from the subscriber, living in Fork of Gunpowder, near Meredith's Ford, Negro Bowie, a likely young fellow, about 5 feet 7 or 8 inches high, 23 years of age, or thereabouts. – He had a down look, and his tongue is so glib that he is nicknamed Lawyer – he is well cloathed, having a jacket and breeches of white kersey, new osnaburg shirt, good yarn stockings, and his shoes plated at the toes – one of his shoes has been cut with an axe from the sole upwards, near where the quarter and vamp join, and has been sewed up. Whoever will secure the said Negro in any gaol, or will deliver him to me, shall have Six Dollars reward, if he is within five miles of home, and Five Pounds, if at the distance of sixteen miles. George Fitzhugh. January 8, 1785." (Ref: *Maryland Journal and Baltimore Advertiser*, 1 Feb 1785)

Negro Lewis. "25 Dollars Reward. – Ran away from the subscriber on Monday, 6th August [1838], a Negro Boy named Lewis, about 17 or 18 years of age, about 5 feet 2 or 3 inches high; had on a Cloth Cap with a Tassel, Osnaburg Pantaloons nearly worn, and a Cotton Shirt. The above reward will be paid for his delivery in Baltimore County Jail. Ann Maria Mitchell, Little Gunpowder, near Joppa." (Ref: *Baltimore American*, 9 Aug 1838)

One Dollar Reward.

Ran away from the subscriber, from on board the Schooner William, now lying at Mc Elderry's wharf, Baltimore, a dark Mulatto BOY, named Lewis, about five feet four or five inches high, had on when he went away a pair of kersey trowsers and roundabout jacket, made out of a drab colored coat. Masters of vessels and others are forbid harboring him at their peril, as they will be dealt with as the rigor of the law will direct. Whoever will take up said boy and secure him in Baltimore goal shall receive the above reward.

JAMES TAYLOR,
Abington, Harford County:

April 1 d4t*

Negro London. "One hundred dollars reward. Ran Away, about the 1st of January 1799, a Negro man, called London, about 5 feet 10 or 11 inches high, rather raw-boned, his voice rather effeminate, has a scar on his forehead and down one side of his face, a cut on or by one of his shins, one on his hand, I believe his right, both with the axe, the scar on his face occasioned by a scald when young, appears rather blacker that his natural colour, had to serve nine years, is very fond of playing the violin. Whoever takes up and secures the said negro, so I get him again, shall receive, if 10 miles twenty dollars, if 20 miles thirty dollars, if 50 miles fifty dollars, if 80 miles seventy dollars, if a hundred miles or more, the above reward, and reasonable charges if brought home, paid by William Hollis, Harford County, Maryland, 24th January, 1800." (Ref: *The Pennsylvania Gazette*, 5 Feb 1800)

Negro Mary. 1830. "William Billingslea, residing 21 miles from Baltimore on the Philadelphia Turnpike Road, offers reward for negro girl, Mary, age 16-17, 5 ft 5-6 inch; had on a iron collar which she can hide with her handkerchief; took with her changes of dress." (Ref: *Independent Citizen*, 21 Oct 1830; *Newspaper Abstracts of Cecil & Harford Counties, 1822-1830*, by F. Edward Wright, 1984, p. 55)

Negro Mary. "$400 Reward. – Ran away from Farm in Harford Co., on night of September 1st [1845], a negro girl Mary, about 20 years old; color black; very short and thick; small hands and feet; flat nose, thick lips; usually combs her wool straight. Also, ran away on July 5, 1845, Negro Man Frisby, about 22 years old; color black; about 5 feet 9 or 10 inches high; upper lip thick and projecting; negro wool; knot on forehead over left eye; large nose, not very flat; walks clumsily, with his toes turned out; joints connecting big toes with feet, very large. These negroes will probably be found together. Provided they are arrested out of the State of Maryland, and I obtain possession of them, I will give the above Reward, or $200 for either, – or $100 for either if arrested in State of Maryland. A Negro Man having absconded for *(sic)* a Neighbour's Farm, at the same time, the above Girl will probably be found with him. Josiah Lee. Baltimore, Sept. 3rd, 1845." (Ref: *Baltimore American and Commercial Daily Advertiser*, 5 Sep 1845)

Negro Mint. "Harford County, March 4, 1780. Two Hundred Dollars Reward. Ran away, from the subscriber, in Bush-River Neck, a Negro Woman, named Mint; had on and took with her a kersey jacket and petticoat, the jacket white, and the petticoat of a brownish yellow, a white linen petticoat, tow linen shift, old shoes and stockings, and some other clothes, is about 25 years of age and has lost some of her upper teeth. Whoever secures her, if in the County, shall have One Hundred Dollars; and if out of the County the above reward, and reasonable charges if brought home, paid by John Hall Hughes." (Ref: *Maryland Journal and Baltimore Advertiser*, 7 Mar 1780)

Harford County, March 4, 1780.

TWO HUNDRED DOLLARS REWARD.

RAN away, from the ſubſcriber, in Buſh-River Neck, a Negro Woman, named MINT; had on and took with her a kerſey jacket and petticoat, the jacket white, and the petticoat of a browniſh yellow, a white linen petticoat, tow linen ſhift, old ſhoes and ſtockings, and ſome other clothes, is about 25 years of age, and has loſt ſome of her upper teeth. Whoever ſecures her, if in the county, ſhall have One Hundred Dollars; and if out of the county the above reward, and reaſonable charges if brought home, paid by

JOHN HALL HUGHES.

Negro Ned. "Four Half Johannes Reward. Ran away, on the night of the 17th instant [April 1781], from the subscriber, living near Susquehannah lower ferry [now Havre de Grace], the two following Negro Men, viz. Davy, a tall slim black fellow, country born, about 23 years of age, upwards of 6 feet high, and lisps in his speech. – Ned, about 35 years of age, country born, about 5 feet 6 or 7 inches high, has full eyes, big legs, and one ankle larger than the other. Both of them have been used to row in the ferry-boats on Susquehannah, and are well known. Their cloathing is country-made tow shirts, and full'd cloth or linsey jacket and breeches; but as they have other clothes, and money, may change their dress. – Any person apprehending both, or either of them, and secures them, so that the subscriber gets them again, shall have, if taken within 10 miles of home, One Half Johannes; if 20 miles, Two Half Johannes; if 30 miles, Three Half Johannes; and if at a greater distance the above Reward, or in proportion for either, and reasonable charges, if brought home, paid by Samuel Thomas. April 21, 1781." (Ref: *Maryland Journal and Baltimore Advertiser*, 24 Apr 1781)

FOUR HALF JOHANNES REWARD.

RAN away, on the night of the 17th instant, from the subscriber, living near Susquehannah lower ferry, the two following Negro Men, viz. DAVY, a tall slim black fellow, country-born, about 23 years of age, upwards of 6 feet high, and lisps in his speech.—NED, about 35 years of age, country-born, about 5 feet 6 or 7 inches high, has full eyes, big legs, and one ankle larger than the other. Both of them have been used to row in the ferry-boats on Susquehannah, and are well known. Their cloathing is country-made tow shirts, and full'd cloth or linsey jacket and breeches; but as they have other clothes, and money, may change their dress.——Any person apprehending both, or either of them, and secures them, so that the subscriber gets them again, shall have, if taken within 10 miles of home, One Half Johannes; if 20 miles, Two Half Johannes; if 30 miles, Three Half Johannes; and if at a greater distance the above Reward, or in proportion for either, and reasonable charges, if brought home, paid by SAMUEL THOMAS.

April 21, 1781.

Negro Neil. "Forty Dollars Reward. Ran away last night [3 Jan 1778] from the subscriber, living near Broad Creek, in Harford County, Maryland, two Negro men, one named Dick, about five feet six or seven inches high, down look, stoop shouldered, small limb; had on and took with him, an half worn felt hat, a tow cloth shirt, a white ditto [i. e., cloth shirt], white plush breeches, speckled stockings, old shoes, and a match coat blanket. The other named Neil, a thick well-made stout fellow, round made, talkative and speaks quick; had on a straw hat, a blue coat with a falling collar, brown thick cloth jacket laced, a tow cloth shirt, white flannel breeches, speckled stockings, and good shoes tied with thongs. Whoever takes up and secures said servants, so that their master may have them again, shall have, if 10 miles from home, ten dollars, if 20 miles twenty dollars, if 30 miles thirty dollars, if 40 miles the above reward, and reasonable charges if brought home, paid by John Barclay." (Ref: *The Pennsylvania Packet*, 21 Jan 1778)

Negro Nero. 1781. "Was delivered to my custody, a Negroe man named Joe, who served ten years with Mr. Jeremiah Strowd, in Barley *(sic)* County, Virginia, says he is now free; likewise a Negroe man, who sometimes says his name is Joe and sometimes Nero, says he lived with Mr. Isaac Webster in Hartford *(sic)* County, Maryland, near Bush-town, and with Mr. Charles Hughes, Antiatum [Antietam], Maryland, and likewise with Mr. William Jones, Maryland. The owner or owners are hereby requested to come, prove their properties, pay costs, and take them away, or they will be sold out for their costs and fees in six weeks from the date hereof. Hugh Cunningham, Goaler [Jailer]. Dec 10 1781. Lancaster County." (Ref: *The Pennsylvania Gazette*, 19 Dec 1781)

Negro Noak. "Ten Dollars Reward. Ran Away, from the subscriber, on the evening of the first instant [June 1790], a Negro Man, named Noak, about 38 years of age, 5 feet 8 or 9 inches high, well-made and of a bold countenance, artful, and very talkative – Had on, and took with him, a coarse linen shirt and trousers, black vest and breeches. It is very probable he may endeavour to pass for a free man, as he attempted it before, and said he was manumitted by Mr. William Amoss. Whoever takes up said slave, or secures him in any gaol, so that the owner may get him again, shall receive, if ten miles from home, Three Dollars; if twenty miles, Five Dollars; if thirty miles, Eight Dollars; and, if forty miles, the above reward, and all reasonable charges, if brought home, paid by Joshua Amoss. Harford County, near the upper Cross Roads, June 10, 1790." (Ref: *Maryland Journal and Baltimore Advertiser*, 11 Jun 1790)

Ten Dollars Reward.

RAN AWAY, from the fubfcriber, on the evening of the firft inftant, a NEGRO MAN, named NOAK, about 35 years of age, 5 feet 8 or 9 inches high, well made and of a bold countenance, artful, and very talkative:— Had on, and took with him, a coarfe linen fhirt and troufers, black veft and breeches. It is very probable he may endeavour to pafs for a free man, as he attempted it before, and faid he was manumitted by Mr. William Amofs. Whoever takes up faid flave, or fecures him in any gaol, fo that the owner may get him again, fhall receive, if ten miles from home, THREE DOLLARS; if twenty miles, FIVE DOLLARS; if thirty miles, EIGHT DOLLARS; and, if forty miles, the above reward, and all reafonable charges, if brought home, paid by

JOSHUA AMOSS.

Harford County, near the upper Crofs Roads,
June 10, 1790

Negro Oliver. "Fifteen Pounds Reward. Ran away on the 4th of October, 1784, from the subscriber, living on Deer Creek, in Harford County, Maryland, a Negroe man, named Oliver, tho' commonly called Nol. He is a well set fellow, about 30 years of age, 5 feet 6 inches high, of a good black colour, a high round forehead, middling large ears and mouth, his feet and legs are of the larger size, with a small scar over and across one of his eye-brows (I think his right eye-brow); had on when he went runaway, a new brown cloth coat with bright buttons, a white jacket, white shirt, and some kind of trowsers, shoes and stockings, with some things in a bundle; he likely will change his name and procure a pass, and endeavour to pass for a free man. He once before ran away, and was taken up in Pennsylvania by the above-described scar. Whoever takes up said fellow, and delivers him to his master, or secures him in any gaol, so that his master may get him again, shall have the above reward, paid by Freeborn Brown. N. B. It is thought there are others in company with him that are also run aways, particularly a stout yellowish fellow. They probably will push to the Jersies. All masters of vessels and others are forewarned from harbouring or carrying him or them off." (Ref: *The Pennsylvania Gazette*, 13 Oct 1784)

The same advertisement was published again later, but with these changes: "He is left-handed ... brown cloth coat with bright-faced buttons ... N.B. It is thought there is a yellowish fellow in company with him, who is also run away, that has been used to the water, and that they might attempt following that profession; and that they will probably make for Pennsylvania, New Jersey, New York or New England ... Freeborn Brown." (Ref: *The Pennsylvania Gazette*, 1 Dec 1784)

Negro Philip. In 1830 Henry Dorsey, son of Edward, of Bel Air, offered rewards for these runaway negroes: Dinah, age about 52, black; Caroline, daughter of Dinah, age about 34; three sons of Caroline: Bob, age 12, Philip, age 10, and, Joe, age 8; Charles, age about 21; Harriet, sister of Charles, age about 23. (Ref: *Independent Citizen*, 30 Sep 1830; *Newspaper Abstracts of Cecil & Harford Counties, 1822-1830*, by F. Edward Wright, 1984, p. 55)

Negro Pompey. "Sixteen Dollars Reward. Ran away, from the subscriber, living on Winter's Run, in Harford County, a Negro Man named Pompey, about 25 years of age, 5 feet 8 or 9 inches high, a well set fellow, has a bold daring look, very artful and shifty, and if taken and not well examined will probably make his escape, as he has lately effected his escape by having a knife concealed in his bosom; Had on and took with him, a country cloth jacket and breeches, the jacket burnt in the lower part of the back, and a piece put in, gray yarn stockings, a pair [of] half-worn shoes, lately capt and sold [soled], a blue regimental coat, turned up with red, a white linen shirt. Whoever takes up and secures the above Fellow, so that his master gets him, shall have, if within the neighbourhood, or 10 miles from home, *Six Dollars*; if out of the County, *Eight Dollars*; and if out of the State, the above Reward, and reasonable charges paid, if brought home, by James Amoss, Jun., Feb. 17, 1783." (Ref: *Maryland Journal and Baltimore Advertiser*, 18 Feb 1783)

SIXTEEN DOLLARS REWARD.

RAN away, from the subscriber, living on Winter's Run, in Harford County, *a Negro Man named POMPEY*, about 25 years of age, 5 feet 8 or 9 inches high, a well set fellow, has a bold daring look, very artful and shifty, and if taken and not well examined will probably make his escape, as he has lately effected his escape by having a knife concealed in his bosom: Had on and took with him, a country cloth jacket and breeches, the jacket burnt in the lower part of the back, and a piece put in, gray yarn stockings, a pair half-worn shoes, lately capt and sold, a blue regimental coat, turned up with red, a white linen shirt. Whoever takes up and secures the above Fellow, so that his master gets him, shall have, if within the neighbourhood, or 10 miles from home, *Six Dollars*; if out of the County, *Eight Dollars*; and if out of the State, the above Reward, and reasonable charges paid, if brought home, by

JAMES AMOSS, jun.

Feb. 17, 1783.

Negro Pompey. "A Runaway Negro Lad. Ran away, from the subscriber's farm, on Deer-Creek, Harford County, on or about the first inst. [1 Nov 1785], a Negro Lad, named Pompey, about 17 years of age, 5 feet 4 or 5 inches high, and has a down look; had on and took with him when he went away, an old felt hat, white country kersey jacket, much worn, a pair of coarse linen trousers, good shoes, and an old gray great coat, which he may have got altered into a jacket, and have changed his dress. He has been very lately seen in Baltimore-Town and on the Point, and may still be lurking about there. Whoever will secure the said Negro Lad, so that his Master can get him again, shall receive Eight Dollars, or if brought home, and delivered to his Overseer, Twelve Dollars Reward will be paid, by John Rumsey. Joppa, Nov. 24, 1785." (Ref: *Maryland Journal and Baltimore Advertiser*, 25 Nov 1785)

A Runaway Negro Lad.

Ran away, from the subscriber's farm, on Deer-Creek, Harford County, on or about the first inst. a *Negro Lad*, named *POMPEY*, about 17 years of age, 5 feet 4 or 5 inches high, and has a down look; had on and took with him when he went away, an old felt hat, white country kersey jacket, much worn, a pair of coarse linen trousers, good shoes, and an old gray great coat, which he may have got altered into a jacket, and have changed his dress. He has been very lately seen in Baltimore-Town and on the Point, and may still be lurking about there.

Whoever will secure the said Negro Lad, so that his Master can get him again shall receive EIGHT DOLLARS, or if brought home, and delivered to his Overseer, TWELVE DOLLARS Reward will be paid, by

Joppa, Nov. 24, 1785. JOHN RUMSEY.

Negro Pompey. "Thirty Dollars Reward. Ran away, from the subscriber, on Friday evening last [December 1786], a Negro Fellow, named Pompey, thick, well made, and about 5 feet 7 or 8 inches high; he had on and took with him when he went away, a new pair of shoes and stockings, a new pair of black and white kersey breeches, two old kersey jackets, the one white, and the other black and white, and an old felt hat, about half worn; his head is remarkably long from the chin to his crown, and a very round scull, a small beard, with a small white speck on each side of his chin; he keeps his wool combed back on the top of his head, forming a toupee; he is very timorous when he has done anything not warrantable, and at that time has a down look, and is constantly, when fitting, working of his foot, and looking down. – Any person taking him up, and bringing him home, shall have, if 10 miles from home, One Dollar; if 20 miles, Three Dollars; if 40 miles, Six Dollars; if 60 miles, Twelve Dollars; and if 100, the above Reward, and all reasonable charges, paid by the subscriber, living on the Bayside, near Susquehannah. Joshua Brown. December 17, 1786." (Ref: *Maryland Journal and Baltimore Advertiser*, 29 Dec 1786)

Thirty Dollars Reward.

Ran away, from the ſubſcriber, on Friday evening laſt, *a Negro Fellow*, named *POMPEY*, thick, well made, and about 5 *feet* 7 *or* 8 *inches* high; he had on and took with him when he went away, a new pair of ſhoes and ſtockings, a new pair of black and white kerſey breeches, two old kerſey jackets, the one white, and the other black and white, and an old felt hat, about half worn; his head is remarkably long from the chin to his crown, and a very round ſcull, a ſmall beard, with a ſmall white ſpeck on each ſide of his chin; he keeps his wool combed back on the top of his head, forming a toupee; he is very timorous when he has done any thing not warrantable, and at that time has a down look, and is conſtantly, when ſitting, working of his foot, and looking down.——Any perſon taking him up, and bringing him home, ſhall have, if 10 miles *from* home, One Dollar; if 20 miles, Three Dollars; if 40 miles, Six Dollars; if 60 miles, Twelve Dollars; and if 100 miles, the above Reward, and all reaſonable charges, paid by the ſubſcriber, living on the Bayſide, near Suſquehannah. JOSHUA BROWN.

December 17, 1786.

Negro Prince. 1790. "Four Dollars Reward. Ran Away, from the subscriber, living in Gunpowder Neck, Harford County, a Negro Man, named Prince, about 5 feet 10 inches high, 26 years of age, has been a ferry-man several years, is a black likely Negro, stammers in his speech, can saw with a cross-cut and whip-saw. Had on, and took away, a fear-nought jacket, a fustian and a cloth coat, brown breeches, black linsey under jacket, nankeen jacket and breeches, and a tow-linen shirt. Whoever apprehends said Negro, and secures him in any gaol, so that I may get him again, shall have Four Dollars reward, and all reasonable charges if brought home, paid by Lambert Wilmer. N. B. It is supposed that said Negro will endeavour to enter on board some vessel, as a hand; therefore, all masters of vessels are fore-warned hiring or carrying him off, at their peril. Feb. 24, 1790." (Ref: *Maryland Journal and Baltimore Advertiser*, 2 Mar 1790)

Four Dollars Reward.

RAN AWAY, from the fubfcriber, living in Gunpowder Neck, Harford County, a NEGRO MAN, named *PRINCE*, about 5 feet 10 inches high, 26 years of age, has been a ferry-man feveral years, is a black likely Negro, ftammers in his fpeech, can faw with a crofs cut and whip-faw: Had on, and took away, a fearnought jacket, a fuftian and a cloth coat, brown breeches, black linfey under jacket, nankeen jacket and breeches, and a tow-linen fhirt. Whoever apprehends faid NEGRO, and fecures him in any gaol, fo that I may get him again, fhall have FOUR DOLLARS reward, and all reafonable charges, if brought home, paid by LAMBERT WILMER.

N. B. It is fuppofed that faid NEGRO will endeavour to enter on board fome veffel, as a hand; therefore, all mafters of veffels are forewarned hiring or carrying him off, at their peril. *February* 24, 1790.

Negro Richard. "West Chester, Chester County, August 2, 1790. Was committed to the gaol of this County, on the 26th of Jul last, two Negroe men, who call themselves Richard and Harry. Richard is about 5 feet 8 inches high, a stout well-made man. Harry is not quite so tall nor so thick built. They are about 30 years old each, and acknowledge themselves slaves of James Amos and Joshua Amos, of

Harford County, Maryland. Their Masters are requested to come, pay charges, and take them away, otherwise they will be sold, to discharge the cost, in four weeks from this Date. Charles Dilworth, Sheriff." (Ref: *The Pennsylvania Gazette* 4 Aug 1790)

"August 14, 1790. Broke away last evening from the constable of Kennet, on their way to Westchester [West Chester] gaol, two Negroe Slaves, belonging to James and Joshua Amos, of Harford County, in the state of Maryland; the one a stout built fellow, about five feet eight or nine inches high, named Richard; the other about five feet six inches high, named Harry, both very black. Whoever apprehends and secures the abovesaid Negroes, so that they may be had, shall have Three Pounds reward for each of them, and reasonable charges, paid by the subscriber, living in Kennet township, Chester County." (Ref: *The Pennsylvania Gazette*, 6 Oct 1790)

Negro Sally. "Harboring Runaway Slaves. – Yesterday afternoon [1 Jan 1841] Mr. Benjamin Rigden [actually Rigdon], of Harford County, was arrested by officers McKeown and Shelden and brought before Justice Jones, charged with harboring two runaway slaves – Sally and her child – the property of Mr. James Wilks, of this city [Baltimore]. It appeared in evidence that some twelve days ago, these blacks left their owners *(sic)* and were not heard of until yesterday, when Mr. Rigden called at the store of the owner and made it known. The sum of $20 was offered, if they were restored. Mr. Rigden, not being satisfied with this, said to some person in the store, as appears from the testimony, that unless he received $100, he would put the negroes over the line into Pennsylvania. It was also proved that he said the negroes were now in his possession. Upon the strength of this evidence, he was held to bail for his appearance at the Baltimore County court in the sum of $800." (Ref: *Baltimore Sun*, 2 Jan 1841)

Negro Sam. "Norristown, Montgomery County [PA], May 1, 1791. Was taken up, on suspicion of being a runaway, and committed to my custody, in Norristown gaol, on the 11th instant, a Negro man, who calls himself Sam, says he is the property of Ralph Bond, of Hartford *(sic)* County, Mary-land, and that he left his master about Christmas last [1790]; he also says his former master's name was Elijah Bozley [actually Bosley], of Maryland. He is a thick square made fellow, about five feet seven or eight inches high, appears to be about 25 or 26 years of age, and is somewhat marked with the pox. The owner is desired to come, prove his property, pay charges, and take him away, within five weeks from the date hereof, otherwise he will be sold, for the charges and cost of imprisonment, by me. William Stroud, Gaoler." (Ref: *The Pennsylvania Gazette*, 18 May 1791)

Negro Samuel. "Seven Hundred and Fifty Dollars Reward. – Ran away from the subscriber, living in Harford County, Md., on Sunday, 27th May last [1855], three Negro Men, named 'James,' 'Talbot,' and 'Samuel.' James is quite black, about 5 feet 9 inches high, good looking, pleasant when spoken to; 35 years old; left a free mulatto wife in the neighborhood; called himself "James Crumwell.' Talbot is a dark mulatto, 23 years old, round face, rather small eyes, 5 ft. 5 inches high, very short neck; had on a rough dark grey coat when he left; called himself 'Talbot Jones.' Samuel, a mulatto, 21 years old, front teeth broad, with a space between; delicately made, 5 ft. 7 inches high, and has a down look when spoken to, and calls himself 'Samuel Jones.' The above reward will be paid for the apprehension of the three negroes, if secured in any jail, so I can get them again, or $250 for either. William Hutchins, Taylor P. O., Harford County, Md." (Ref: *Baltimore Sun*, 4 Jul 1855) [William is buried in St. James P. E. Church Cemetery.]

Negro Santy. An old black man named Santy ran away from Thomas A. Hays of Bel Air in May 1861. Hays offered a $50 reward for the slave's return. (Ref: *National American*, 7 Jun 1861)

Negro Santy. 1861. "Runaway Negroes. Four negro men, George, Charles, Santy and Alex, belonging to Thomas A., Hays, Esq., of this place [Bel Air], left home on Sunday morning last [2 Jun 1861], to go fishing, as they said, but the last heard of them they had taken the cars at Perryville, opposite Havre-de-Grace, for Philadelphia. The negro man who conveyed them across the river at Havre-de-Grace has been arrested and is now in Bel Air jail. – They applied at the ticket office, we learn, on Sunday for tickets to Philadelphia, but being refused them, they loitered about Perryville for some time, when by some means they got on the train for Philadelphia and went off. The Railroad Company being informed of the facts, immediately telegraphed the intelligence to that place.

"The mule belonging to their master and the horse and carriage which they hired from citizens of Bel Air, by which to make their escape, they left in Havre-de-Grace.

"Four hundred dollars reward is offered for the arrest of the four men and the delivery of the property which they took with them.

"Mr. Hays has also offered two hundred dollars for the arrest of a negro man names Sam, who ran away one year ago, and fifty dollars for another, (old negro), named Santy, who went away about three weeks ago." (Ref:

National American, 7 Jun 1861)

Negro Sauntee. "100 Dollars Reward. Ran-away from the subscriber, living in Harford County, three miles from Belle-Air, on Monday, 30th July [1810], a negro man named Sauntee, who calls himself Sauntee Marshel, between 24 and 25 years of age, about five feet six or seven inches high; of a yellow complexion; slow speech; wide mouth; good teeth; flat nose, and a smiling shy countenance when spoken to; one of his fingers on the left hand crooked, occasioned by a hurt in the middle joint of the finger; he also has a knot swelled on one of his wrists, about the size of a robin's egg, near the joint; a very small beard, wears his hair tied behind; and bends somewhat back; had on a ticklenburg shirt and trousers, and a dark striped vest; his other clothing not recollected. The above reward will be paid for the said negro if taken out of the State, fifty dollars if taken out of the County, and twenty dollars if taken in the County, and reasonable charges of brought home, paid by William H. Sewall." (Ref: *Daily National Intelligencer*, 23 Aug 1810)

Negro Smith. "The Fatal Occurrence at Columbia, Pa. The news by telegraph has already informed the public of a fatal occurrence which took place in Columbia, Pa. On Wednesday [28 Apr 1852]. Some of the parties have since arrived in this city [Baltimore], from which the following particulars have been obtained. It appears that Archibald G. Ridgely, of the firm of Zell & Ridgely, on Wednesday last, left this city for the purpose of arresting two runaway slaves, the alleged property of Messrs. George W. Hall and H. B. Michael, of Harford County, Md., he first obtaining powers of attorney of these gentlemen. He proceeded to Harrisburg, Pa., and there obtained a warrant of the commissioner of that district, went to Columbia, where the runaways were engaged at work. He was accompanied to Columbia by two deputy marshals. Shortly after getting there, they learned that one of the negroes, named Smith, said to be the property of Mr. Hall, was employed at a lumber yard ... [remainder of the article is missing from my copy]. (Ref: *Baltimore Sun*, 1 May 1852)

Negro Stepney. "Fifty Dollars Reward. Ran away, from the Subscriber, living in Harford County, near Spesutia Church, a Negro Man, named Stepney, a Shoemaker by Trade, 37 or 38 Years of Age, 5 feet 7 or 8 inches high, a black Fellow, and has lost one of his fore Teeth out of his upper Jaw, has a small Scar at the Corner of his Eye; he took with him a blue Broadcloth Coat, a Kersey Jacket, some white and tow-linen Shirts, one Pair of striped Trousers and a Leather Hat. He is an artful Fellow, and probably may endeavour to pass for a free Man. Any Person delivering said Fellow to the Subscriber, if apprehended in the County, shall receive *Fifteen Dollars*; if out of the County, and above 30 miles from Home, *Eighteen Dollars*; if 40 miles, *Twenty-one Dollars*, and so in Proportion; and if 100 miles from Home, the above reward, if secured in Gaol so that his Owner may get him again, or if brought Home, reasonable Charges, paid by Josias Hall. Harford County, Oct, 1, 1784." (Ref: *Maryland Journal and Baltimore Advertiser*, 22 Oct 1784)

FIFTY DOLLARS REWARD.

RAN away, from the Subſcriber, living in Harford County, near Spefutie Church, a NEGRO MAN, named STEPNEY, a Shoemaker by Trade, 37 or 38 Years of Age, 5 Feet 7 or 8 Inches high, a black Fellow, and has loſt one of his fore Teeth out of his upper Jaw, has a ſmall Scar at the Corner of his Eye; he took with him a blue Broadcloth Coat, a white Kerſey Jacket, ſome white and Tow-Linen Shirts, one Pair of ſtriped Trouſers and a Leather Hat. He is an artful Fellow, and probably may endeavour to paſs for a free Man. Any Perſon delivering ſaid Fellow to the Subſcriber, if apprehended in the County, ſhall receive *Fifteen Dollars*; if out of the County, and above 30 miles from Home, *Eighteen Dollars*; if 40 miles, *Twenty-one Dollars*, and ſo in Proportion; and if 100 Miles from Home, the above Reward, if ſecured in Gaol ſo that his Owner may get him again, or if brought Home, reaſonable Charges, paid by

Harford County, Oct. 21, 1784. JOSIAS HALL.

Negro Suck. "Forty Dollars Reward. Run away from the subscriber, in King and Queen County, Virginia, about the first of November last [1783], two Virginia born Negroes, by the names of Isaac and Suck. Isaac is about 40 years of age, 6 feet high, of a yellowish complexion, with a scar over one of his eyes, and one of his arms has been broke just above the wrist. Suck is about 30 years of age, 5 feet high, very black, with one of her teeth out before, which is perceivable. They carried away different clothes with them, and a small black horse, which they stole from Virginia; their aim was Philadelphia, and I expect have gone there, as they were taken up on the main road from Baltimore to Philadelphia, in Harford County, Maryland, but made their escape. Whoever apprehends and secures the said Negroes in any goal [jail], or gives information, so that I may get them again, shall receive the above reward, paid by William Dew." (Ref: *The Pennsylvania Gazette*, 10 Dec 1783)

Negro Talbot. "Seven Hundred and Fifty Dollars Reward. – Ran away from the subscriber, living in Harford County, Md., on Sunday, 27th May last [1855], three Negro Men, named 'James,' 'Talbot,' and 'Samuel.' James is quite black, about 5 feet 9 inches high, good looking, pleasant when spoken to; 35 years old; left a free mulatto wife in the neighborhood; called himself "James Crumwell.' Talbot is a dark mulatto, 23 years old, round face, rather small eyes, 5 ft. 5 inches high, very short neck; had on a rough dark grey coat when he left; called himself 'Talbot Jones.' Samuel, a mulatto, 21 years old, front teeth broad, with a space between; delicately made, 5 ft. 7 inches high, and has a down look when spoken to, and calls himself 'Samuel Jones.' The above reward will be paid for the apprehension of the three negroes, if secured in any jail, so I can get them again, or $250 for either. William Hutchins, Taylor P. O., Harford County, Md." (Ref: *Baltimore Sun*, 4 Jul 1855)

Negro Thomas. "One Hundred and Fifty Dollars Reward. – Ranaway from the subscriber, living in Harford County, Md., on the night of the 3rd inst. [June 1843], a negro man named Thomas, aged about 25 years, six feet 1 or 2 inches high, straight and well made; when spoken to answers pleasantly, and with a smile; there is no marks by which he can be more minutely described. He took several suits of clothes with him; amongst which 1 blue frock coat, 1 check do [coat], 1 linen jacket, 1 pair blue cassinett pants, 1 mix'd gambroon do [pants], 1 silk vest, 1 pair fine boots, 1 white hat. It is supposed he had made his way to Pennsylvania, as two other slaves went from the same neighborhood the same night. The above reward will be paid upon delivery at the Harford or Baltimore County jail, so that I can get him again. Jesse Jarrett." (Ref: *Baltimore Sun*, 10 Jun 1843)

ONE HUNDRED AND FIFTY DOLLARS REWARD.—Ranaway from the subscriber, living in Harford county, Md., on the night of the 3d inst., a negro man named THOMAS, aged about 25 years, six feet 1 or 2 inches high, straight and well made; when spoken to answers pleasantly, and with a smile; there is no marks by which he can be more minutely described. He took several suits of clothes with him; amongst which was 1 blue frock coat, 1 check do, 1 linen jacket, 1 pair blue cassinett pants, 1 mix'd gambroon do, 1 silk vest, 1 pair fine boots, 1 white hat. It is supposed he has made his way to Pennsylvania, as two other slaves went from the same neighborhood the same night. The above reward will be paid upon delivery at the Harford or Baltimore county jail, so that I can get him agin.

je10-ws6t* JESSE JARRETT.

Negro Tom. Letter dated 24 Oct 1834 from John Whisner in Philadelphia to William M. Maclaskey, in care of Dr(?) William J. McElhiney, Bel Air, Harford County. "Dear Sir, I suppose you think strange for not hearing from me sooner but the men who gave me this information where your man Tom lived was taken up soon after giving the information and I have never been able to see him since till this day and he says he will show him to me at any time I will go with him. Tom is about 20 miles from this place; there is no doubt of this information being correct as I got it from Mrs. Gallup's Mike some years since. Tom is of the description you gave and a fiddler and fond of liquor and idle. You also wish to know my lowest terms with all persons I do business for. I have one hundred and fifty dollars for taking a slave and the owner paying all expenses except the spy and the constable or one half they will bring in Maryland after all our expenses are deducted out of the sale or I will give one hundred and twenty-five dollars and I will pay all expenses of those proposals I give choice. There is also a fellow in the same neighborhood and came from your County about the same time your Tom came, he is also a yellow fellow and belongs to Mr. William Brooks of Harford County, his name at home was Ephraigm. If Mr. Brooks wishes him taken and will come or send me a power of attorney and a witness, I will take him on the same terms that I offered to take Tom for. You will please to see Mr. Brooks or let me know on the receipt of this what post office Mr. Brookes *(sic)* lives near. You will keep this information a secret at home to prevent the negro getting information as there are men in your neighborhood that would write on to the Quakers and give information. Let me hear from you soon. Yours respectfully, John Whisner, at 39 Quince Street between Ham---(?) and Locust and Spruce Sts. N.B. If you send a power of attorney be particular to have it drawn up in a proper form. J. W." On the back of the envelope: "J. G. Hoffner, No. 229 South Sixth Street, Matlock--[smudged] at Woodbury, a friend." (Ref: Historical Society of Harford County, Archives Dept.)

Negro Tombo. "Three Pounds Reward. Absented himself from Otter-Point Ship-Yard, the 1st instant [January 1784], Negro Tombo, by trade a calker, he is upwards of six feet high, and well set, one of his legs is a little larger than the other; he has an uncommon limp in his walk, from a complaint in his hip – The clothes he had on were his ordinary working clothes, made of striped blanketing; he borrowed a small black horse, which it is probable he has sold. If he is not in the County, it is supposed he is lurking about Fell's-Point [in Baltimore], or perhaps gone to Philadelphia, in both of which places he has been accustomed to work at his trade. – Whoever will apprehend him and secure him in any gaol, so that the owners may get him, shall have the above Reward, and reasonable charges if returned to the Yard, paid by Francis Holland and Co. Harford County, Jan, 28, 1784." (Ref: *Maryland Journal and Baltimore Advertiser*, 17 Feb 1784)

THREE POUNDS REWARD.

Abſented himſelf from Otter-Point Ship-Yard, the 1ſt inſtant, NEGRO TOMBO, by trade a calker, he is upwards of ſix feet high, and well ſet, one of his legs is a little larger than the other; he has an uncommon limp in his walk, from a complaint in his hip---The clothes he had on were his ordinary working clothes, made of ſtriped blanketing; he borrowed a ſmall black horſe, which it is probable he has ſold. If he is not in the county, it is ſuppoſed he is lurking about Fell's-Point, or perhaps gone to Philadelphia, in both of which places he has been accuſtomed to work at his trade.——Whoever will apprehend him and ſecure him in any gaol, ſo that the owners may get him, ſhall have the above Reward, and reaſonable charges if returned to the Yard, paid by

FRANCIS HOLLAND and CO.

Harford County, Jan. 28, 1784.

Negro Will. 1789. "Jacob Bond and Robert Dutton of near Joppa, Harford County, advertised for 'Negro Man Will, age 25.' He 'took along two horses, and wife 18 or 20, two boys about five and two.' He 'had forged pass, made towards little York.' The woman and children were the property of Dutton, and Will belonged to Bond. Slavery was no respecter of family ties." (Ref: "York County Slavery," by June Lloyd, posted on www.yorkblog.com, 21 Apr 2013)

Negro William. "Received June 2nd 1819 from Mr. Archer Hays six dollars for printing Handbills and for advertising Negro William 4 weeks in the Lancaster Journal. [signed] Willm. Hamilton." (Ref: Historical Society of Harford County, Archives File "Slavery-Runaways"). [Archer Hays (1755-1827)'s stone mansion, built in 1808, and his spring house down the hill in front of the house, are now on the campus of Harford Community College near Bel Air.]

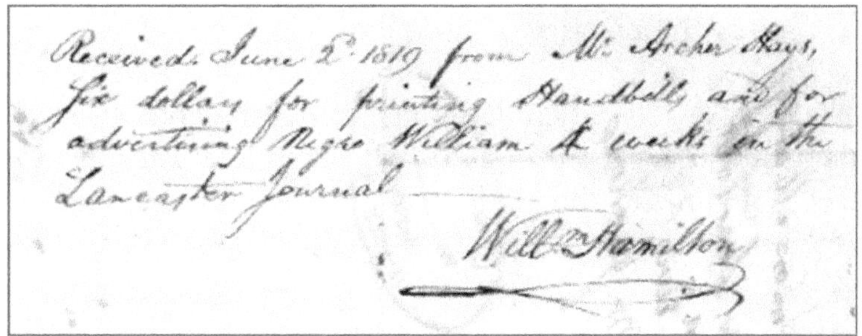

Received June 2d 1819 from Mr Archer Hays,
Six dollars for printing Handbills and for
advertising Negro William 4 weeks in the
Lancaster Journal

Will Hamilton

Nowland, Ned. “Four Hundred Dollars Reward. – Ran away from the subscriber, on Saturday night, 23rd inst. [1851], Two Boys. Ned Nowland is 5 feet 10 inches high; 20 years old; chesnut *(sic)* color; has a scar on the cheek bone (not recollected which). He wore a black coat and pantaloons; he took a bundle of other clothing with him. Thomas Billingslea is 5 feet 6 inches high; 21 years old; black; clothing the same as the other. The above reward will be given for both, or $200 for either, if lodged in some jail so I may get them again. Washington M. Slade, Harford County, Maryland, near Abingdon post-office.” (Ref: *Baltimore Sun*, 27 Aug 1851)

Owens, James Henry. “Twenty Dollars Reward. – Ran away from the subscriber, on the 27th of Dec. last [1844], a bright mulatto Boy between 14 and 15 years old, and bound to me until he is 21. He is a smart, good-looking boy, and can be easily detected by his right leg being sore, it has been sore for 18 months, is offensive, a disease of the bone, and in all probability will not be well for 2 or 3 years. He has free relations in Baltimore, and was with them from the time he ran away from me until the 16th of January, 1844, since which time I have not heard from him. He has relations at Ellicott's Mills also, and lived there 4 or 5 years, with a barber. I think it likely he is secreted somewhere in that part of the country, if he is not in the city. I will give $10 if taken in the city of Baltimore, and $20 if taken out of the city and lodged in jail (and all reasonable expenses paid) so that I get him again. All persons are forewarned harboring him, at their peril. Wm. T. Munnikhuysen, Bel Air, Harford County, Md." (Ref: *Baltimore American*, 8 Feb 1844)

TWENTY DOLLARS REWARD.—Ranaway from the subscriber, on the 27th of Dec. last, JAS. HENRY OWENS, a bright mulatto Boy, between 14 and 15 years old, and bound to me until he is 21. He is a smart, good looking boy, and can be readily detected by his right leg being sore, it has been sore for 18 months, is offensive, a disease of the bone, and in all probability will not be well for 2 or 3 years. He has free relations in Baltimore, and was with them from the time he ranaway from me until the 16th of January, 1844, since which time I have not heard of him. He has relations at Ellicott's Mills also, and lived there 4 or 5 years ago, with a barber. I think it likely he is secreted somewhere in that part of the country, if he is not in the city. I will give $10 if taken in the city of Baltimore, and $20 if taken out of the city and lodged in jail (and all reasonable expenses paid) so that I get him again. All persons are forewarned harboring him, at their peril.

WM. T. MUNNIKHUYSEN,

feb 8 eo3t* Bel Air, Harford county, Md.

Parks, Jack. "Five Hundred Dollars Reward. Ran away from the subscribers, living near Joppa, Harford County, Md., on Saturday, 28th of July last [1841], Three Negro Men, calling themselves Phil Dixon, Ben Dixon, and Jack

Parks. Phil is about 35 years old, 5 feet 10 inches high, of a corpulent make, very dark, has a dull speech, and has lost some of his front teeth. Ben is about 30 years old, 5 feet 8 or 9 inches high, of a slender appearance, pleasant address, and very polite when spoken to. Jack is about 40 years old, 5 feet 10 or 11 inches high, has a pleasant appearance when spoken to, and is very dark. The above reward will be given for the apprehension of the above negroes, or a proportional reward for either, if taken within this State or elsewhere, and lodged in jail so that the owners may get them again. C. W. Hatton. Catherine Parks." (Ref: *Baltimore Sun*, 6 Sep 1841)

Presbury, Stephen. "May Term 1845. We the Grand Inquest of the State of Maryland for the body of Harford County, do on our Oaths present Phebe Presbury, a free Negro woman, for enticing and persuading away from the premises of the late John Wilson, a negro boy named Stephen Presbury, bound to the said Wilson, according to Law, as an Apprentice on or about the 15th day of May, 1845, against the peace, dignity and government of the State. John McGaw, Foreman. John Whitaker, Witness." (Ref: Historical Society of Harford County, Court Records Document 112.13.2A)

Prigg vs. Pennsylvania, see Margaret Morgan.

Rawlings, Charles. "Notice. – Was committed, on the 13th day of June, 1823, to the jail of Baltimore County, as a runaway, a black negro man, by the name of Charles Rawlings, who says he belongs to William Hall, of Harford County; he is 5 feet 6 inches high, about 21 years of age; had on when committed, dark gray pantaloons, blue coat, white vest, fine hat, coarse shoes and stockings. The owner of the above-described negro is desired to come forward, prove property, pay charges, and take her *(sic)* away, or she *(sic)* will be otherwise be discharged accordingly to law. Sheppard C Leakin, Sheriff of Balt. Co." (Ref: *Daily National Intelligencer*, 24 Jul 1823)

Rhoades, Charles. In the August 1861 term of the Circuit Court of Harford County, "Charles Rhoades, a free negro, at said term, convicted of assisting negroes to run away, the said sentence directing the said free negro to be sold for a period of 8 years, as and for a slave to the purchaser for and during said term, I hereby give notice that on Tuesday, the 15th day of October, 1861, I will exposed to public sale, at the Court House door in Bel Air, to the highest bidder for cash, the said Charles Rhoades, free negro, which when sold will become the property of the purchaser for and during the period of eight years, as aforesaid. Charles Rhoades is about thirty years of age, about five feet seven or eight inches high, and in a sound and healthy condition. Sale to be take place between the hours of twelve and two o'clock P. M. Joseph E. Bateman, Sheriff, Harford County." (Ref: *The Southern Aegis*, 28 Sep 1861). [He was listed on the criminal docket in 1861. (Harford County Criminal Docket Book, 1858-1863). This appears to have been the Charles Rhoads, age 34 in 1860, born in Maryland, laborer, who was head of household with Rebecca, age 20, Mary, age 4, and Georgiana, age 1. (1860 Harford Co. Census)]

Rice, Hull. "$600 Reward. – Ran away from the subscribers' Farms, in Harford County, on Saturday night, September 3rd [1842], the following described Negroes: Harriet Demby, 23 years old, colour black, thick lips, forehead full, very small hands and small feet and ears, wool fine, and when well combed nearly straight, a little below medium stature, speaks low. Among her clothing were four Calico dresses, various colours, a black and white Straw Bonnet trimmed with pea green ribbon, a cross-bar scarlet and green Blanket Shawl, Worked Collars, Capes and Wrist Cuffs. Hull Rice, 28 years old, colour black, medium stature, very erect, pleasant address, very little beard, lisps slightly. The above Negroes were engaged to be married, and now, doubtless, live together as Man and Wife. George Stewart, 28 years old, dark Mulatto or copper colour, below medium stature, small head, awkward form and manner, short Negro hair, and very little beard, speaks remarkably quick. The above Slaves have probably crossed the Susquehanna River at some point between Port Deposite [actually Deposit] and Columbia Bridge. We will give $200 for the apprehension of either or the same sum for each. Charles W. Lee, Churchville, Harford County, Md. Josiah Lee, Baltimore." (Ref: *Baltimore American and Commercial Daily Advertiser*, 7 Sep 1842)

Ringgold, Charles. "Arrival from Maryland [into Philadelphia], 1859. Jim Kell, Charles Heath, William Carlisle, Charles Ringgold, Thomas Maxwell, and Samuel Smith ... Charles Ringgold was eighteen years of age; no white blood showed itself in the least in this individual. He fled from Dr. Jacob Preston, a member of the Episcopal Church, and a practical farmer with twenty head of slaves. 'He was not so bad, but his wife was said to be a 'stinger.' Charles left his mother and father behind, also four sisters.

"Charles Ringgold took offence at being whipped like a dog, and the prospect of being sold further South; consequently in a high state of mental dread of the peculiar institution, he concluded that freedom was worth suffering for, and although he was as yet under twenty years of age, he determined not to remain in Perrymanville, Maryland, to wear the chains of Slavery for the especial benefit of his slave-holding master (whose name was inadvertently omitted)." (Ref: *The Underground Railroad*, by William Still, 1871, repr. 1970, pp. 521-523). [There was a Charles Ringold born in April 1841, son of William and Mary Ringold, who was baptized on 10 Jul 1848 at St. George's Protestant (Spesutia) Episcopal Church in Perryman. (Ref: St. George's P. E. Church Register, 1834-1903)]

Rogers, Isaac. "$100 Reward. Ran away from the subscriber, on Saturday, the 27th ult. [27 Feb 1858], a negro man named Isaac Rogers. He is about 26 years of age, has a scar over the left eye, and walks lame, as if his leg had been broken. He is about 5 feet 4 or 5 inches high, medium black, and was dressed in a black jacket and drab pants, coarse shoes, and white slouch hat. The above reward will be paid if he is lodged in jail, so that I can obtain possession of him. Isaac German, Harford Road, Balt. Co." (Ref: *The Southern Aegis*, 27 Mar 1858)

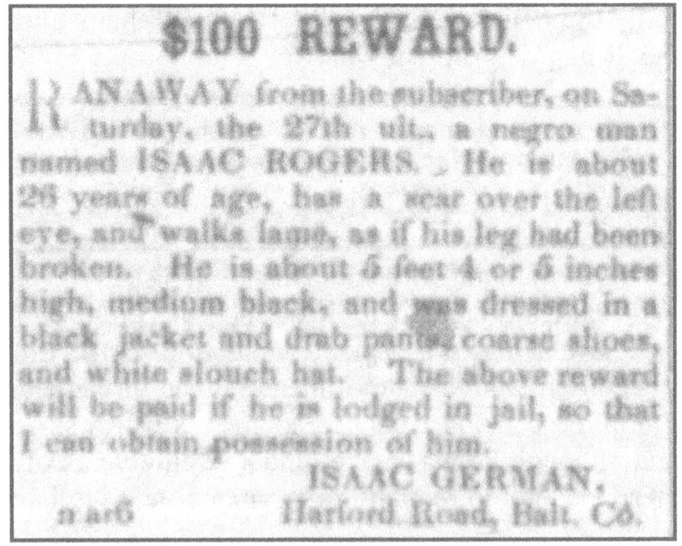

$100 REWARD.

RANAWAY from the subscriber, on Saturday, the 27th ult., a negro man named ISAAC ROGERS. He is about 26 years of age, has a scar over the left eye, and walks lame, as if his leg had been broken. He is about 5 feet 4 or 5 inches high, medium black, and was dressed in a black jacket and drab pants, coarse shoes, and white slouch hat. The above reward will be paid if he is lodged in jail, so that I can obtain possession of him.

ISAAC GERMAN,

mar6 Harford Road, Balt. Co.

Rollins, Charles. "Notice. – Was committed to the jail of Baltimore County, on the 5th day of February, 1825, by Thomas Baily, Esq., a Justice of the Peace of the city of Baltimore, a negro man, who says his name is Charles Rollins, and belongs to Wm. Sappington and George Winham, of Havre de Grace, Md.; he is 5 feet 5½ inches high, about 22 years of age; had on when committed, a blue cloth jacket, silk vest, blue cassinet pantaloons, linen short, fur hat, and shoes and stockings. The owner of the above-described negro is desired to come forward, prove property, pay charges, and take him away, or he will be otherwise be discharged accordingly to law. S. Barry, Shff. B. C." (Ref: *Daily National Intelligencer*, 15 Feb 1825)

Rope Ferry Incident. "During the summer of 1841, three young African Americans of Harford County, Maryland, decided that life as slaves was unendurable. Under the harsh Maryland slave codes, it was unlikely they would ever be freed by their owners or able to purchase their freedom. The only viable option was to run, and they made their plans accordingly.

"The young men were Alick, and the brothers Ben and Tom. Their surnames are unknown at present. Alick, age 21, was owned by John C. C. Hall [actually John Carvil Cranberry Hall]. Ben and Tom were owned by Mr. Hall's brother, George O. D. Hall [actually George Josias Ontario Hall]. The Hall brothers had inherited the slaves as part of their deceased father's estate. It is likely that the three slaves were cousins. Alick was described as strong, healthy, able to play a fiddle and a strong Methodist.

"Alick, Ben and Tom left the Hall brothers' property on or about July 4, 1841. Since this was a holiday, they probably chose it as a day when their presence (or lack thereof) would not be immediately noticed. giving them a twenty-four-hour head start. About the 6th of July they were missed, and the Hall brothers took action, writing powers of attorney to each other. In addition, they prepared an advertisement for the missing slaves which they left with their local postmaster. Such advertisements included complete descriptions of runaways, including the clothing they were wearing when last seen.

"The Halls engaged the services of Jonathan McVey [1810-1895, buried in Zion Methodist Church Cemetery in Cecil Co., MD], a local slave hunter who started on the chase immediately. Harford County borders York County, Pennsylvania on the north, and the Susquehanna River and Chesapeake Bay on the east and south. John Hall met McVey at Havre ed Grace (at the mouth of the Susquehanna). They travelled north from there, knowing that there were much frequented 'freedom routes' along the eastern bank of the Susquehanna, through Cecil County, Maryland, into Lancaster County, Pennsylvania.

"McVey and Hall proceeded up the Susquehanna to Columbia. Just as a network existed to assist fugitive slaves, there was also a network of those who profited by hunting them. McVey must have had contacts in this network for he was able to determine that the three men had been sent west along the canal from the Harrisburg area to the Juniata River instead of continuing north along the Susquehanna River.

"Accordingly, at Martin's Tavern, described in the court case as 'five miles beyond Harrisburg,' and a place mentioned where the fugitives had been seen, he hired Richard Black, a resident of Perry County, to assist in the 'rescue' of the slaves. Black, who lived at Clark's Ferry, could tap into the Perry County network of slave hunters and informers. At this point Hall decided the hunt was in good hands, gave the powers of attorney, and a certain amount of cash to McVey. He then returned home to Harford County, Maryland.

"Richard Black, in turn, recommended John Toland of Miller Township, located northwest across the Juniata River from Clark's Ferry, as another man with local contacts. The three slave hunters continued on horseback toward Newport, a town on the west bank of the Juniata River and a port on the canal.

"Meanwhile, Alick, Ben, and Tom reached Newport on the morning of Thursday, July 8th, 1841. They were more than one hundred miles north of Harford County. Since they traveled this distance in four days, it is possible they moved by canal boats for some of the distance. Underground Rail-road contacts in Columbia, Wrightsville, and Harrisburg would have aided them. Once in Newport, they talked to Colonel William Kibler, who kept a hotel near the canal. Apparently, using Underground Railroad contacts, they must have been told to look for Kibler once they reached Newport. Kibler offered them a chance to earn some money in the relative safety of Newport, and the three went to work on a house being built near Kibler's hotel or tavern,

"Sometime in the afternoon, there thee slave hunters rode into Newport. The young men at Kibler's were alerted at once and, after grabbing their coats, left town going north following the canal towpath. Black and Toland were recognized in Newport, and excitement must have crackled through the quiet riverside town.

"A group of men and boys headed north along the canal with the three slave hunters. Among this group was Captain John W. Bosserman and several other man who would later be arrested and charged with the federal crime of preventing a slave owner from recovering his property.

"Alick, Ben, and Tom did not realize the towpath ended at Rope Ferry, and they became trapped between the river and the canal. The slave hunters were about 300 yards behind them, and the crowd of townsmen was between the pursuers and the fugitives. Toland rushed ahead of the crowd and fired his pistol into the air when Ben dove into the river to swim across it. Supposedly, Toland yelled at him not to go into the water. It is unknown if Toland knew Ben could not swim. The coroner's report stated Ben had drowned, and there was no mention of a gunshot wound. However, the rumor spread quickly through town that Ben had been shot to death.

"Alick and Tom were captured by Black, McVey, and Toland. In the meantime, a canal boat had come downstream, and crossed the river on the continuous rope pulley. The three slave hunters and two surviving fugitives were taken on board ..."

"The two runaways were imprisoned at Newport, but when it came time to leave Alick and Tom could not be found. In the meantime, subsequent to the 1842 trial, "newspaper accounts state that Mr. Bosserman and several other Newport men of similar convictions told Alick and Tom that they were free to go. Furthermore, they took up an impromptu monetary collection for them and told them what route to take. More than likely they were told where to find assistance between Newport and Lewistown." (Ref: *African Americans in Perry County: 1820-1925*, by Janet Taylor, 2011, pp. 45-52, which tells the rest of the story)

On 10 Oct 2012 Janet Taylor, of Carlisle, PA, wrote to author, genealogist, and local historian Henry C. Peden, Jr. in Bel Air, MD, as follows: "Dear Mr. Peden, Thank you for your prompt rely to my query regarding the fugitives from Harford County in 1841. Although I know it is extremely difficult to recover the surnames of slaves, I have been successful in at least one case, so continue to live in hope! I do have some further information on this case and am happy to share it with you.

"First of all, I am author of the recently published book, 'African Americans in Perry County: 1820-1925.' I am enclosing the title page and chapter concerning the Rope Ferry Incident involving the three young men from Harford County, I am currently preparing an article on the subject for further publication When it is finished, I will forward it to you.

"It appears from your findings and the testimony at the case of Hall vs. Monroe (Eastern District Court October 18-22, 1842) there was considerable obfuscation concerning the actual ownership of these young men. Your findings indicate Tom was the property of George Hall. Sworn testimony indicated Ben and Tom were brothers, and George Hall owned them both.

"The Hall brothers claimed they didn't know who owned Alick, but John Hall tried to have him arrested, claiming he was Alick's owner. I am not surprised *Hunter Sunderland's Slave Manumission and Sales in Harford County, Maryland 1775-1865* has no information about these transactions since they seem to have been done in an extra-legal manner, probably for the purpose of tax evasion. (My research has found that tax evasion was rampant in Cumberland-Perry Counties from 1750 to 1840, and I cannot believe it was not widespread.)

"The judge's findings were not available, but it appears only the case of Tom, whose actual ownership could be more or less determined, was considered. The defense realized they would lose the case, so concentrated on under-mining and ridiculing the evidence and testimony of the plaintiff's legal team. The defense asked for a lenient ruling and got it. A fine of $2000 was levied against all ten defendants, reducing the individual liability to $200. Tom was never recovered by George Hall.

"Tom and Alick were escorted to the western edge of Newport, close to where the capture of the three men occurred. The townsmen present gave them money to continue their journey and advised them where assistance could be found. It seems likely they were directed up the Juniata River to the town of Lewistown. From there the likely route was across the Seven Mountains into Centre County, up the West Branch of the Susquehanna to Sinnemahoning Creek and thence into western New York State reaching the crossing into Canada at Niagara.

"It is possible the two young men chose to remain in Pennsylvania or New York. There were communities of free African Americans willing to shelter them. Even Perry County, as close to the Maryland and Virginia borders as it was, had communities of former slaves. The Underground Railroad was alive and well throughout south central Pennsylvania."

"Thank you for your prompt attention to my query. Should I find any further information about Tom and Alick, I will share it with you. Sincerely, Janet L. Taylor." (2012)

Schley, Belinda Sophia. "One Hundred Dollars Reward. – Absconded from the subscriber in the Spring of 1841, a Black Girl, who formerly and probably still goes by the name of Belinda Sophia Schley, but who has within the few years, been married to a colored man by the name of Graves; she is about 30 years of age, has usually rather a down look, but when spoken to she puts on quite a fierce-look; she is well known in Baltimore, having been hired to some of the principal Hotels there, viz: Page's Exchange Hotel, the Eutaw House, and Barnum's City Hotel, and more frequently to Randal H. Moale, Esq., J. C. Moale,

Esq. and Jos. Owens, Esq. She is small of stature, and dark colored; it is not recollected that she has any mark about her except a scar on one of her thumbs, occasioned by a burn; she has been frequently of late in Baltimore, where it is supposed she has been ever since she left the place where she was last hired with my consent; and all persons are hereby warned against hiring or harboring her without a written order from me. I will pay the above reward if taken out of the State, or Fifty Dollars if taken in the State, and out of the City of Baltimore, or Twenty-five Dollars if taken in the city of Baltimore and secured so that I get her again. Martha Robinson, Bel Air, Aug. 10 1842." (Ref: *Baltimore Sun*, 13 Aug 1842)

Scott, Hetty. "Hetty Scott, alias Margaret Duncans, and daughter Priscilla. [1853]. This mother and daughter had been the 'chattels personal' of Daniel Coolby [Cooley?] of Harvard *(sic)*, Md. Their lot had been that of ordinary slaves in the country, on farms, &c. The motive which prompted them to escape was the fact that their master had 'threatened to sell' them. He had a right to do so, but Hetty was a little squeamish on this point and took great umbrage at her 'kind master.' In this 'disobedient' state of mind, she determined, if hard struggling would enable her, to defeat the threats of Mr. Daniel Coolby [Cooley?], that he should not much longer have the satisfaction of enjoying the fruit of the toil of herself and offspring. She at once began to prepare for the journey.

"She had three children of her own to bring, besides she was intimately acquainted with a young man and a young woman, both slaves, to whom she felt that it would be safe to confide her plans with a view of inviting them to accompany her. The young couple were ready converts to the eloquent speech delivered to them by Hetty on

Freedom, and were quite willing to accept her as their leader in the emergency. Up to the hour of setting out on their lonely and fatiguing journey, arrangements were being carefully completed, so that there should be no delay of any kind. At the appointed hour they were all moving northward in good order.

"Arriving at Quakertown, Pa., they found friends of the slave, who welcomed them to their homes and sympathy, gladdening the hearts of all concerned. For prudential reasons it was deemed desirable to separate the party, to send some one way and some another. Thus safely, through the kind offices and aid of the friends of Quakertown, they were duly forwarded on to the Committee in Philadelphia. Here similar acts of charity were extended to them, and they were directed on to Canada." (Ref: *The Underground Railroad*, by William Still, 1871, repr. 1970, pp. 205-208)

There is a discrepancy in the aforementioned story. On 25 Nov 1853 it was recorded that the master's name was David Coobly. She "left last May and went to Quakertown where they have been ever since. Was brought to this city [Philadelphia] by Henry Franklin. Hetty's owner had been threatened *(sic)* to sell her and her child, the fear of which prompted them to escape. So, she got herself & 3 children, and two of her neighbour's children (young men & women) ready and escaped the doom that hung over her head. The owner of this family was particularly severe. Expences: $4.37." (Ref: *Journal C of Station No. 2 of the Underground Railroad, Agent William Still, 1852-1857.* Vigilance Committee of Philadelphia, Pennsylvania Anti-Slavery Society, Pennsylvania Abolition Society Papers, Historical Society of Pennsylvania)

Scott, Harry. "$100 Reward. – Ran away from the subscriber, living in Harford County, on Saturday the 6th inst. [July 1835] a Negro Man named Harry, sometimes goes by the name of 'Harry Scott.' He is a dark yellow, about 6 feet one or two inches high, and well made, supposed to have a scar on one of his hands occasioned by a burn; he is a first-rate farm hand. He had on when he went away a blue cloth coat, mazarine blue pantaloons, and took a variety of other clothing with him; he is supposed to have forged a pass. The above reward will be given if taken and secured so that I can get him again, and all reasonable charges paid if brought to the subscriber. Aquila Hall, Hall's Mill. Near Bush Town, Harford County, Md." (Ref: *Baltimore American*, 20 Jun 1835)

$100 REWARD.—Ranaway from the subscriber, living in Harford County, on Saturday the 6th inst. a Negro Man named HARRY, sometimes goes by the name of "Harry Scott." He is a dark yellow, about 6 feet one or two inches high, and well made, supposed to have a scar on one of his hands occasioned by a burn; he is a first rate farm hand. He had on when he went away a blue cloth coat, mazarine blue pantaloons, and took a variety of other clothing with him; he is supposed to have forged a pass. The above reward will be given if taken and secured so that I can get him again, and all reasonable charges paid if brought to the subscriber.

AQUILA HALL, Hall's Mill.
Near Bush Town, Harford County, Md.

Smith, Edward. "Arrival from Belle Air [into Philadelphia in 1858]. Julius Smith, Wife Mary, and Boy James, Henry and Edward Smith, and Jack Christy. While this party was very respectable in regard to numbers and enlisted much sympathy, still they had no wounds or bruises to exhibit, or very hard reports to make relative to their bondage. The treatment that had been meted out to them was about as tolerant as Slavery could well afford; and the physical condition of the passengers bore evidence that they had been used to something better than herring and corn cake for a diet.

"Of this party, Edward, a boy of seventeen, called forth much sympathy; he too was claimed by Hollan [Robert W. Holland]. He was of a good physical make-up, and seemed to value highly the great end he had in view, namely, a residence in Canada." (Ref: *The Underground Railroad*, by William Still, 1871, repr. 1970, pp. 473-474)

Smith, Henry. "Arrival from Belle Air [into Philadelphia in 1858]. Julius Smith, Wife Mary, and Boy James, Henry and Edward Smith, and Jack Christy. While this party was very respectable in regard to numbers and enlisted much sympathy, still they had no wounds or bruises to exhibit, or very hard reports to make relative to their bondage. The treatment that had been meted out to them was about as tolerant as Slavery could well afford; and the physical condition of the passengers bore evidence that they had been used to something better than herring and corn cake for a diet.

"Henry was about twenty-three years of age, of an active turn, brown skin, and had given the question of freedom his most serious attention, as his actions proved. While he could neither read nor write, he could think. From the manner in which he expressed himself, with regard to Robert Hollan [Robert W. Holland], no man in the whole range of his recollections will be longer remembered than he; his enthrallment while under Hollan will hardly ever be forgotten. Any being who had been thus deprived of his rights, could hardly fail to command sympathy; in cases like this, however, the sight and language of such a one was extremely impressive." (Ref: *The Underground Railroad*, by William Still, 1871, repr. 1970, pp. 473-474)

Smith, John. 1858. He "was a yellow boy, nineteen years of age, stout build, with marked intelligence. He held Dr. Abraham Street responsible for treating him as a slave. The doctor lived at Marshall District, Harford County, Maryland. John frankly confessed, to the credit of the doctor, that he got 'plenty to eat, drink and wear,' yet he declared that he was not willing to remain a slave, he had higher aims; he wanted to be above that condition. 'I left,' said he, 'because I wanted to see the country. If he had kept me in a hogshead of sugar, I wouldn't have stayed,' said the bright-minded slave youth. 'They told me anything – told me to obey my master, but I didn't mind that. I am going off to see the scripture,' said John. (Ref: *The Underground Railroad*, by William Still, 1871, repr. 1970, p. 541)

Smith, Julius. "Runaway Negroes. Our town [Bel Air] was thrown into a considerable excitement on Monday morning last [21 Mar 1858], by the intelligence that a batch of negroes had decamped from their owners, and were on their way to Pennsylvania. As far as heard from, there were six in the party, three men belonging to Robert W. Holland, Esq., one man belonging to Mrs. Lee, and a woman and child belonging to Henry W. Archer, Esq. It appears that on Sunday afternoon about four o'clock, one of the negroes hired a wagon of one of our citizens, to which was attached one of Mr. Holland's mules, apparently for a little ride, since which time nothing has been heard of them.

"Early on Monday morning a posse of the town, headed by Sheriff Whiteford, proceeded in the direction of the Pennsylvania line, near which they found the mule and wagon in a fence corner. It is supposed, from the rapid appearance of the river and the heavy wind which prevailed on Sunday night, that the party failed in crossing, hence there is a reasonable prospect that some of them at least being apprehended.

"Mr. Holland immediately offered a reward of $1000 for the arrest of his boys, who are very valuable to him, and who had been indulged to such an extent as to preclude all suspicion of any attempt or disposition to leave. There is no doubt but the party had accomplices in their schemes, and a sharp look should be kept by our people to discover the lurking places of these wolves in sheep's clothing, that they may receive a merited punishment. There is another warning too, to our officers of justice, to see that all the laws relating to negroes are strictly carried out, particularly those relating to their meeting together on secret societies – one of which we understand exists in our village at this very time." (Ref: *The Southern Aegis*, 27 Mar 1858)

"Arrival from Belle Air [into Philadelphia]. Julius Smith, Wife Mary, and Boy James, Henry and Edward Smith, and Jack Christy. While this party was very respectable in regard to numbers and enlisted much sympathy, still they had no wounds or bruises to exhibit, or very hard reports to make relative to their bondage. The treatment that had been meted out to them was about as tolerant as Slavery could well afford; and the physical condition of the passengers bore evidence that they had been used to something better than herring and corn cake for a diet.

"Julius, who was successful enough to bring his wife and boy with him, was a wonderful specimen of muscular proportions. Although a young man, of but twenty-five, he weighed two hundred and twenty-five pounds; he was tall and well-formed from the crown of his head to the soles of his feet. Nor was he all muscle by a great deal; he was well balanced as to mother wit and shrewdness.

“In looking back into the pit from whence he had been delivered he could tell a very interesting story of what he had experienced, from which it was evident that he had not been an idle observer of what had passed relative to the Peculiar Institution; especially was it very certain that he had never seen anything lovely or of good report belonging to the system. So far as his personal relations were concerned, he acknowledged that a man named Mr. Robert Hollan [Robert W. Holland], had assumed to impose himself upon him as master, and that this same man had so wrongly claimed all his time, denied him all common and special privileges; besides he had deprived him of an education, etc., which looked badly enough before he left Maryland, but in the light of freedom, and from a free State standpoint, the idea that 'man's inhumanity to man' should assume such gigantic proportions as to cause him to seize his fellow-man and hold him in perpetual bondage, was marvellous *(sic)* in the extreme.

“Julius had been kept in the dark in Maryland, but on free soil, the light rushed in upon his astonished vision to a degree almost bewildering. That his master was a man of 'means and pretty high standing' – Julius thought was not much to his credit since they were obtained from unpaid labor. In his review allusion was made not only to his master, but also to his mistress, in which he said that she was 'a quarrelsome and crabbed woman, middling stout.' In order to show a reason why he left as he did, he stated that 'there had been a fuss two or three times' previous to the escape, and it had been rumored 'that somebody would have to be sold soon.' This was what did the mischief so far as the 'running away' was concerned. Julius' color was nearly jet black, and his speech was very good considering his lack of book learning; his bearing was entirely self-possessed and commendable.

"His wife and boy shared fully in his affections, and seemed well pleased to have their faces turned Canada-ward. It is hardly necessary to say more of them here." (Ref: *The Underground Railroad*, by William Still, 1871, repr. 1970, pp. 473-474)

Smith, Samuel. "Arrival from Maryland [in Philadelphia], 1859. Jim Kell, Charles Heath, William Carlisle, Charles Ringgold, Thomas Maxwell, and Samuel Smith … Sam has been tied up and beat many times severely." Nothing further was written about him. (Ref: *The Underground Railroad*, by William Still, 1871, repr. 1970, pp. 521-522)

Smith, William Henry. "$25 Reward. – Ran away from the subscriber, on Tuesday, 31st ult. [December 1844], a colored boy named Wm. Henry Smith, alias Gibbs, 18 years old, 5 feet 6(?) inches high, slender made, dark chesnut *(sic)* color, and has a pleasant address. Had on a plaid cassinett frock coat and pants, and black shirt. He is well acquainted in this city [Baltimore]. He took with him a sorrel mare, 4 years old – [illegible wording] – and a normal(?) star in her forehead. I will pay $15 for the apprehension of said boy, without the horse, and $10 for the horse, or the above reward for both, if delivered to me. Shedrack Street, near Jarrettsville, Harford County, Md." (Ref: *Baltimore Sun*, 4 Jan 1845)

"$25 Reward. – Ran away from the subscriber, on Wednesday, 12th inst. [November 1845] from the team on the road to Baltimore, near the first gate on the Harford Road, a Negro Boy by the name of Wm. Henry Smith, alias Gibbs, between 18 and 19 years old, 5 feet 9 or 10 inches high, copper color, and had on an old fur cap, red and drab coat and new home-made pants. The above reward will be paid for his return to me, near Jarrettsville, Harford County, or lodged in jail so that I may get him again. Shedrach Street." (Ref: *Baltimore Sun*, 13 Nov 1845)

Stansbury, Charlotte. "Was committed to the Jail of Baltimore City and County, on the 19th day of July, 1833, by Charles Kernan, Esq., a Justice of the Peace, in and for the City of Baltimore, as a runaway, a mulatto woman who calls herself Charlotte Bond or Stansbury; says she belongs to Mrs. Mary Smithson living in Harford County near Belair. Said mulatto woman is about 35 years of age, 4 feet 9 1-2 inches high, has a scar on her right thumb caused by the cut of an axe, also, one on her left arm by being scratched by a cat. Had on when committed, a blue and yellow calico frock, blue and red handkerchief on her head, black silk handkerchief on her neck, check apron and old pair of shoes. The owner of the above-described mulatto woman is requested to come forward, prove property, pay charges and take her away, otherwise she will be discharged according to law. D. W. Hudson, Warden, Baltimore City and County Jail." (Ref: *Commercial Chronicle and Daily Intelligencer*, 29 Jul 1833)

Stewart, George. "$600 Reward. – Ran away from the subscribers' Farms, in Harford County, on Saturday night, September 3rd [1842], the following described Negroes: Harriet Demby, 23 years old, colour black, thick lips, forehead full, very small hands and small feet and ears, wool fine, and when well combed nearly straight, a little below medium stature, speaks low. Among her clothing were four Calico dresses, various colours, a black and white Straw Bonnet trimmed with pea green ribbon, a cross-bar scarlet and green Blanket Shawl, Worked Collars, Capes and Wrist Cuffs. Hull Rice, 28 years old, colour black, medium stature, very erect, pleasant address, very little beard, lisps slightly. The above Negroes were engaged to be married, and now, doubtless, live together as Man and Wife. George Stewart, 28 years old, dark Mulatto or copper colour, below medium stature, small head, awkward form and manner, short Negro hair, and very little beard, speaks remarkably quick. The above Slaves have probably crossed the Susquehanna River at some point between Port Deposite [actually Deposit] and Columbia Bridge. We will give $200 for the apprehension of either or the same sum for each. Charles W. Lee, Churchville, Harford County, Md. Josiah Lee, Baltimore." (Ref: *Baltimore American and Commercial Daily Advertiser*, 7 Sep 1842)

Turner, Joshua. "Twenty Dollars Reward. – Ran away from the subscriber, living in Harford County, Md., on Thursday, the 18th inst. [May 1843], a Negro Boy by the name of Joshua Turner, about 15 years of age; rather thick set, and has one of his front teeth out. Had on when he left a straw hat, linen pantaloons, drab homemade jacket. The above reward will be paid for his arrest by securing him in jail so that I may get him again, or by applying or addressing a letter to Mrs. Sarah Grafton, Hickory P. O., Harford County, Md." (Ref: *Baltimore Sun*, 25 May 1843)

Unnamed Mulatto Boy. 1837. "Runaway. Was committed to Harford County jail on the 30th day of October last [1837], a Dark Mulatto Boy, about 21 years of age, 5 feet, six inches high, very stout made, slow to speak when spoken to. Had on when committed, old woolen clothes, no shoes. Says he belongs to Joseph Hart, living on Miller's Island, Patapsco Neck, Baltimore County, Maryland. John Carsins, Sheriff. Nov. 9, 1837. The Baltimore American and Patriot, will insert the above 3 times." (Ref: *The Madisonian and Harford and Baltimore Advertiser*, 21 Dec 1837)

RUNAWAY.

WAS committed to Harford county jail on the 30th day of October last, a Dark Mulatto Boy, about 21 years of age, 5 feet, six inches high, very stout made, slow to speak, when spoken to. Had on when committed, old woolen clothes, no shoes. Says he belongs to Joseph Hart, living on Millar's Island, Patapsco Neck, Baltimore County, Maryland.

JOHN CARSINS, *Sheriff.*

November 9, 1837.

The Baltimore American and Patriot, will insert the above 3 times.

Unnamed Negro Boy. Letter dated 28 Sep 1841 written by George Hughes in Lancaster, PA to Henry Stump or Widow Stump in Darlington, Harford County, MD: "You have a black boy about 3 miles from the City, if you come on and get him – as the boy is almost in rags – I have understood the boy has about 2 years to serve yet – the boy was enticed away by a white man – otherwise he would not have left – it would be charity for you to bring him home – Mr. Wiley and myself have been at expence, in sending down to you – if you wish to have him we will get him for you for $30 – he must be worth a $100 to you for the term of –?-- years." (Ref: Historical Society of Harford County Archives Dept.)

Unnamed Negro Girl. "Eight Dollars Reward. Ran Away last night [8 May 1789] from the subscriber, at Mr. Jacob

Slagle's, three miles from Hanover [PA], a likely well grown Negro Girl, about fourteen years of age, quite black, soft spoken, round face, very flat feet. She had on new tow linen bed gown, petticoat and shift, and new shoes. Whoever takes up said Negro, and secures in any gaol, so that the subscriber may get her, shall have six dollars, and if carried to Bellair, Harford County, Maryland and delivered to Jacob Norres [Norris], shall have the above reward and reasonable charges. Nathan Gallion. May 9, 1789." (Ref: "Some Slaves got away in York County," by June Lloyd, posted on www.yorkblog.com, 25 Apr 2013)

Unnamed Negroes. "Francis Stokes and his brother Joseph when young men, while walking up the tow path from Lapidum about 1850, saw, lodged in one of these spillways, two slaves chained together by their wrists and drowned, having attempted no doubt to escape from their master." (Ref: *Historical Sketches of Harford County, Maryland*, by Samuel Mason, Jr., 1955, p. 61)

Unnamed Negroes. "Strangers Taken In. – On Friday last [29 Aug 1851], two gentlemen arrived here [Baltimore] from Harford County, Md. (one of whom is named Slade), having each lost a slave, they having absconded towards Baltimore. They stopped at Mr. Hutchinson's Hotel, Front Street, and shortly afterwards came across a fellow who represented himself as a police officer. They soon bargained with him to arrest the negroes for a joint fee of $20, which was paid the pretending officer in the meantime boasting of his great success and sagacity in ferreting out and arresting runaways. Since the operation the fellow has not been heard of. He is, no doubt, an impostor, as he gave an assumed name and failed to meet them according to promise." (Ref: *Baltimore Sun*, 1 Sep 1851)

Unnamed Negroes. "Returned. Two negro men, belonging to John S. Dallam and the other to Henry Nelson, ran away some two months since [January 1864], and after trying for a time the practical workings of the Emancipation Proclamation, came to the conclusion that the kitchens of Mr. Dallam and Mr. Nelson were about the best and most comfortable quarters which they could find, and the other day returned voluntarily to their allegiance." (Ref: *The Aegis & Intelligencer*, 18 Mar 1864)

> RETURNED.—Two negro men, one belonging to John S. Dallam and the other to Henry Nelson, ran away some two months since, and after trying for a time the practical workings of the Emancipation Proclamation, came to the conclusion that the kitchens of Mr. Dallam and Mr. Nelson were about the best and most comfortable quarters which they could find, and the other day returned voluntarily to their allegiance.

Ward, James. "$200 Reward – Ran away from the subscriber on the 24th inst. [August 1836] a negro man named James Ward – he is about 25 years of age, nearly 6 feet high – yellow complexion – a smith by trade, and has been working in this city [Baltimore] for the last 3 years, and it is supposed will make for Pennsylvania. I will give the above reward to any person that will secure him in any jail so that I get him or deliver him to the subscriber living in Bel-Air, Harford Co. Maryland. W. J. McElhenny." (Ref: *Baltimore American*, 30 Aug 1836)

Washington, George. "Dec 5/54. Arrived [in Philadelphia] James Williams, old name Geo. Washington – arrived from Harford Co., Bellair, Md. His owner was named William Fenandus [Farnandis], farmer. James is 19 years of age, chesnut *(sic)* color. Left because his owner talked of selling him. Had been treated as well as could be expected, except the threat of sale." (Ref: *Journal C of Station No. 2 of the Underground Railroad, Agent William Still, 1852-1857.* Vigilance Committee of Philadelphia, Pennsylvania Anti-Slavery Society, Pennsylvania Abolition Society Papers, Historical Society of Pennsylvania)

Washington, Mark. "Sept. 2/54. Arrived [in Philadelphia] Mark Washington, new name Wm. Wilson; complexion dark chesnut *(sic)* color, size medium, age 27 [29?]. Had been owned by James Worthington of Hall's Cross Roads, Md. *(sic)* [Harford] Co., Md. Mark had been treated hard by his owner for which he was induced to leave. He had heard of Canada & freedom & having no expectations of gaining short of Canada he let out. He left a large family behind consisting of his parents, bros. & sisters. To 1 shirt $0.37½, To 1½ days board .75, Washing 2 shirts .12½ [total] $1.25" (Ref: *Journal C of Station No. 2 of the Underground Railroad, Agent William Still, 1852-1857.* Vigilance Committee of Philadelphia, Pennsylvania Anti-Slavery Society, Pennsylvania Abolition Society Papers, Historical Society of Pennsylvania)

Washington, Stephen. "One Hundred Dollars Reward. – Ran away from the subscriber, residing in Harford County, Md., on the 23rd inst. [May 1846], a Negro [boy] who calls himself Stephen Washington. The said boy is about nineteen years old, five feet seven or eight inches high, rather light complexion, and very affable and pleasant when spoken to. The said boy had on when he started a black dress coat, and black pantaloons, but which he has no doubt changed, as he carried with him some variety. Fifty dollars will be given for the apprehension of said boy, if taken within the State, and the above reward if taken without the State, and confined in some jail so that I get him again. Jas. W. Shekell." (Ref: *Baltimore Sun*, 27 May 1846)

Wheeler, Henry. He escaped to Philadelphia circa 1858 with Sydney Hopkins. "These young men made their way out of Slavery together. While Sydney lives, he will forever regard Jacob Hoag, of Havre de Grace, as the person who cheated him out of himself, and prevented him from becoming enlightened and educated.

"Henry, his companion, was also from Havre de Grace. He had had trouble with a man by the name of Amos Barnes, or in other words Barnes claimed to own him, just as he owned a horse or a mule, and daily controlled him in about the same manner that he would manage the animals above alluded to. Henry could find no justification for such treatment. He suffered greatly under the said Barnes, and finally his eyes were open to see that there was an Underground Rail Road for the benefit of all such slavery-sick souls as himself. So, he got a ticket as soon as possible, and came through without accident, leaving Amos Barnes to do the best he could for a living. This candidate for Canada was twenty-one years of age, and a likely-looking boy." (Ref: *The Underground Railroad*, by William Still, 1871, repr. 1970, p. 514)

White, James Henry. "Was Committed to Harford County Jail as a runaway, on the 20th of July, 1859, a Negro Man, very black, about 25 years of age, and about 5 feet 8 or 10 inches high; had on blue cotton pants, a small white hat, and calls himself James Henry White. Any person knowing the above-described negro to be a runaway, will notify me of the same, or otherwise, he will be discharged according to law. Michael Whiteford, Sheriff of Harford County." (Ref: *National American*, 5 Aug 1859). James White was released from jail on 12 Aug 1859, having successfully proven that he was a free man and not a runaway slave. (Harford County General Entries Book TSB No. 6, p. 205)

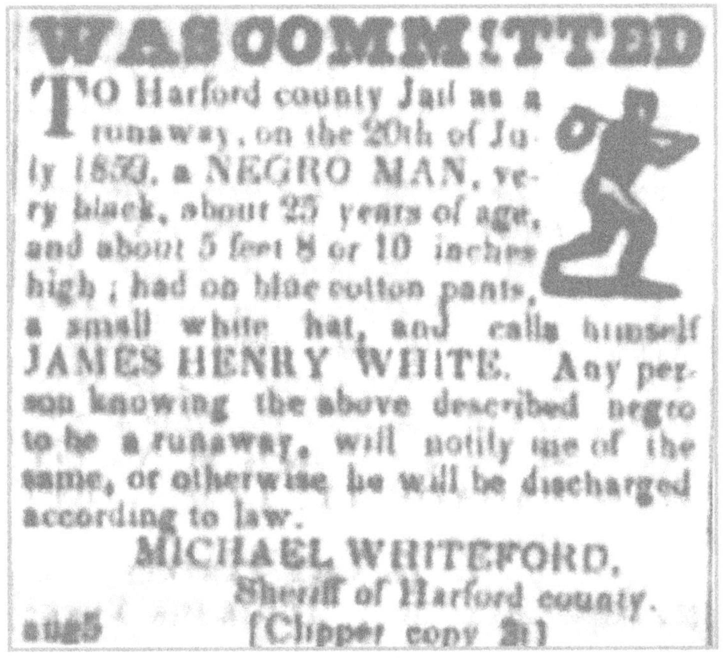

WAS COMMITTED

TO Harford county Jail as a runaway, on the 20th of July 1859, a NEGRO MAN, very black, about 25 years of age, and about 5 feet 8 or 10 inches high; had on blue cotton pants, a small white hat, and calls himself JAMES HENRY WHITE. Any person knowing the above described negro to be a runaway, will notify me of the same, or otherwise he will be discharged according to law.

MICHAEL WHITEFORD,
Sheriff of Harford county.

au5 [Clipper copy 3t]

Williams, Bill. "250 Dollars Reward. Went Away on Saturday, Aug. 31st [1839], a Negro Man called Bill Williams. – about 40 years of age, about feet 9 or 10 inches high, rather dark mulatto, stout, well made, and very likely and intelligent for a negro. He has made wrought nails, is an excellent farm hand, but would be a smart servant in almost any capacity. He took besides other clothing a dark frock coat, dark striped casinet pantaloons, &c. If taken in Maryland and brought here I will give Thirty Dollars – if taken out of Maryland and lodged in any jail in Maryland so that I get him again I will give Two Hundred and Fifty Dollars. John Jay, near Hall's X Roads, Ha. Co. Md. Phil. U.S. Gazette and the Elkton Courier will publish to the amount of $2 each and charge this office." (Ref: *Baltimore American*, 14 Sep 1839)

250 DOLLARS REWARD.

WENT AWAY on Saturday, Aug. 31st. a NEGRO MAN called BILL WILLIAMS,—about 40 years of age, about 5 feet 9 or 10 inches in high, rather dark mulatto, stout, well made, and very likely and intelligent for a negro. He has made wrought nails, is an excellent farm hand, but would be a smart servant in almost any capacity. He took besides other clothing a dark frock coat, dark striped cassinet pantaloons, &c. If taken in Maryland and brought here I will give Thirty Dollars—if taken out of Maryland and lodged in any jail in Maryland so that I get him again I will give Two Hundred and Fifty Dollars.

JOHN JAY,
near Hall's X Roads, Ha. Co. Md.

se 6 lawtt*

☞ Phil. U. S. Gazette and the Elkton Courier will publish to the amount of $2 each and charge this office.

Williams, David. 1839. "$50 Reward. Ran away from the residence of the subscriber, near Bel Air, Harford County, in July last, a negro boy, named David Williams. Said negro is about 18 years of age, square built, about 5 feet 4 inches high. His color is very black and skin remarkably smooth – has rather a sullen countenance. Had on when he went away, a coarse linen roundabout and pantaloons, with a straw hat, with a pink ribbon around it. Whoever takes up dais boy, and lodges it – Bel Air Jail shall receive the above reward. Jane Maulsby. Bel Air, Oct. 15, 1839." (Ref: *Port Deposit Rock*, 31 Dec 1839)

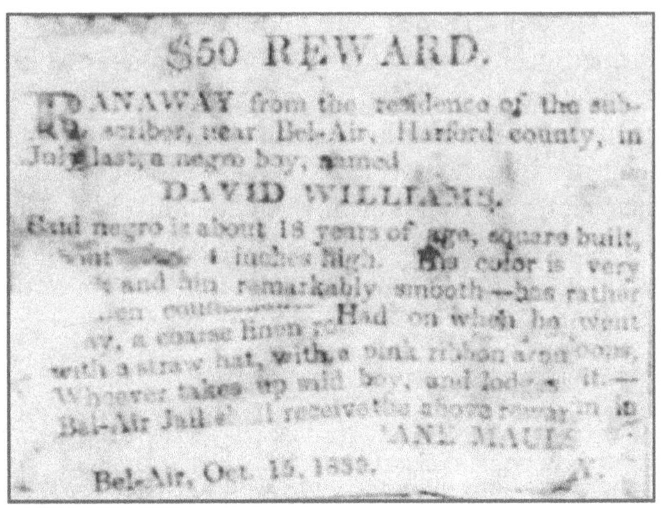

$50 REWARD.

RANAWAY from the residence of the subscriber, near Bel-Air, Harford county, in July last, a negro boy, named

DAVID WILLIAMS.

Said negro is about 18 years of age, square built, [illegible] inches high. His color is very [illegible] and skin remarkably smooth—has rather [illegible] Had on when he went [illegible], a coarse linen [illegible] with a straw hat, with a pink ribbon around it.—Whoever takes up said boy, and lodges it in Bel-Air Jail [illegible] receive the above reward [illegible]

[illegible]

Bel-Air, Oct. 15, 18[illegible].

Wilson, Beck. "$100 Reward. – Ran away from the subscriber, living near the Darlington Post Office, Harford County, Md., on the night of the 28th of December, 1843, a Negro Girl, named Beck Wilson, about 16 years of age – a dark mulatto; she has a double eye-tooth; and when spoken to mumbles some; stout and tall for her age; and good looking. She took with her a variety of clothing; she has a father named Shem Wilson, living with Mr. John Guyton, on the York turnpike, about 18 miles from Baltimore; he is free. If taken in this State, and lodged in any jail that I can get her again, a reward of $50 will be given – if out of the State, $100. Thomas C. Stump." (Ref: *Baltimore Republican and Daily Argus*, 6 Jan 1844)

Wilson, Eliza. 1857. "Harford County, to wit. William H. Stritehoff by Henry W. Archer his Attorney sues Thomas C. Stump for that said Defendant on the fifth day of October in the year 1857 promised to pay to said Plaintiff two hundred dollars if he the said Plaintiff would secure the said Defendants negro woman called Eliza Wilson in the

Baltimore Slave Prison so that said Defendant shall get her in his possession without any further cost within forty-eight hours. And the said Plaintiff avers that he did secure the said negro woman of said Defendant in the Baltimore Slave Prison so that said Defendant got her in his possession without an further cost within forty-eight hours, but said Defendant has not paid said sum of money or any part thereof.

"2nd. And the said Plaintiff also sues the said Defendant for that a certain woman named Eliza Wilson the slave of the said Defendant having runaway and escaped from the said Defendant, the said Plaintiff at the said Defendant's request arrested and secured and delivered her for said Defendant in a Slave Prison in Baltimore City so that said slave was restored to the possession of said Defendant and the said Defendant promised to pay said Plaintiff therefor the sum of $100.

"3rd. And the said plaintiff also sues the said Defendant for that a certain woman named Eliza Wilson the slave of the said Defendant having runaway and escaped from the said Defendant, the said Plaintiff at the said Defendant's request arrested and secured and delivered her for said Defendant in a Slave Prison in Baltimore City so that said Slave was returned to the possession of said Defendant, and the said Defendant promised to pay the said Plaintiff for his services in the premises as much as they were worth.

"4th. And said Plaintiff also sues said Defendant for work and labor, care, diligence and attention by the said Plaintiff done and bestowed for the said Defendant at his request.

"5th. And for money paid, laid out and expended by the said Plaintiff for the said Defendant at his request.

"And the said Plaintiff claims and sues for $400.

Henry W. Archer, Plaintiff's Attorney. Filed 1 May 1858." (Ref: Historical Society of Harford County, Court Records Document 131.0.1)

Wilson, James. 1854. "We take pleasure in apprizing Mr. George Davis, of Harford Co., Md., of the safe arrival of James Wilson and child, claimed by him as his property, and better still, to assure him that they are now safely on the Canadian side of our noble Ontario." (Ref: *Frederick Douglass' Paper*, 1 Sep 1854)

Worl, John. "Notice! Was committed to the Jail of Harford County, on the 27th of November, 1857, as a Runaway, a Negro Man, who calls himself John Worl. He is about 30 or 35 years of age, copper color, and says he is free, and belongs and was raised in Kent County, Maryland. The owner of the above-described Negro is hereby notified to come forward, and prove him, or he will be discharged by due course of law. J. A. Gover, Sheriff. Nov. 20, 1857." (Ref: *National American*, 4 Dec 1857)

NOTICE!

WAS committed to the Jail of Harford county, on the 27th of November, 1857, as a Runaway, a *Negro Man*, who calls himself JOHN WORL. He is about 30 or 35 years of age, copper color, and says he is free, and belongs and was raised in Kent county, Maryland. The owner of the above described Negro is hereby notified to come forward, and prove him, or he will be discharged by due course of law. J. A. GOVER,
Nov. 30, 1857. (d4) Sheriff.

African-American Indentured Servant Runaways, 1863-1882

Barton, William. "Five Cents Reward. Ran away from the subscriber, on the 14th of February, 1869, William Barton, colored, an indentured apprentice. The public are hereby warned not to harbor said boy, under the penalty of the law. John Walter Streett." (Ref: *The Aegis & Intelligencer*, 26 Feb 1869). [This may have been William Y. Barton (b. 1857) who was enumerated in the household of Isaac Barton in 1860. (Harford County Census)]

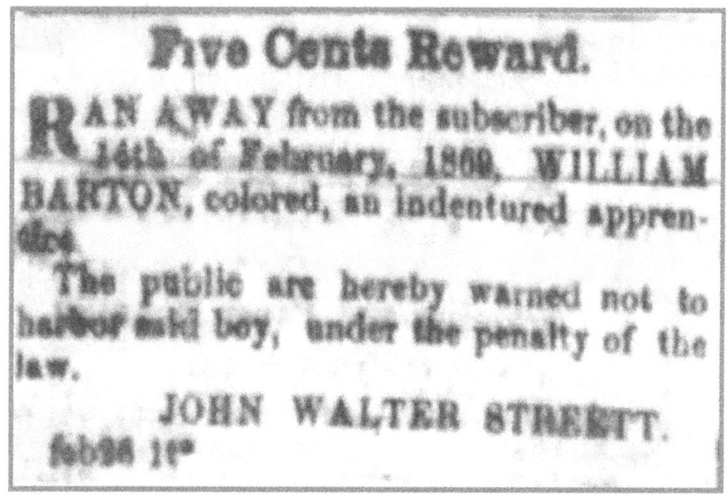

Five Cents Reward.

RAN AWAY from the subscriber, on the 14th of February, 1869, WILLIAM BARTON, colored, an indentured apprentice.

The public are hereby warned not to harbor said boy, under the penalty of the law.

JOHN WALTER STREETT.

feb26 1t*

Cook, Rose. "Five Cents Reward. Ran away from the subscriber, on Sunday, August 4th, 1878, a Colored Girl named Rose Cook, about 11 years old. The above Reward will be paid for her return. All persons are warned not to harbor or trust her on my account. Julia Berry." (Ref: *The Aegis & Intelligencer*, 9 Aug 1878)

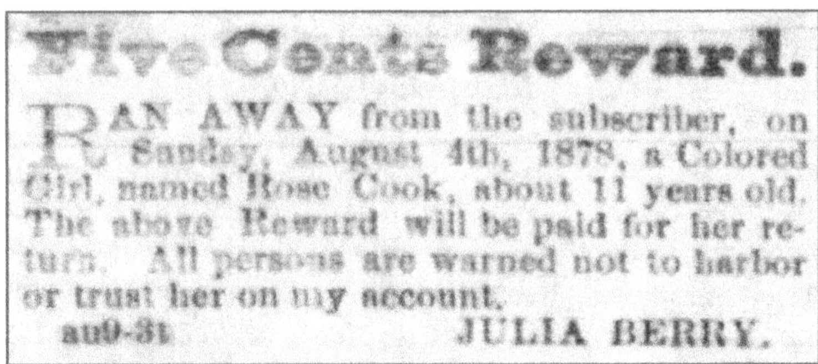

Five Cents Reward.

RAN AWAY from the subscriber, on Sunday, August 4th, 1878, a Colored Girl, named Rose Cook, about 11 years old. The above Reward will be paid for her return. All persons are warned not to harbor or trust her on my account.

au9-3t JULIA BERRY.

Cooper, Steven Henry. "5 Cent Reward. Ran away from the subscriber on Tuesday, January 13th, 1874, bound boy, Steven Henry Cooper, colored, aged eighteen years. When he went away, he was dressed in a grey suit of clothing, with a slouch hat and heavy boots. The above reward will be paid for his return or information of his whereabouts. David Norris, near Fountain Green, Harford Co., Md." (Ref: *The Aegis & Intelligencer*, 23 Jan 1874)

5 Cents Reward.

Ran away from the subscriber on Tuesday, January 13th, 1874, bound boy, Steven Henry Cooper, colored, aged eighteen year. When he went away he was dressed in a grey suit of clothing, with a slouch hat and heavy boots. The above reward will be paid for his return or information of his whereabouts.

DAVID NORRIS,
near Fountain Green Harford Co., Md.
jan23-3t*

Gage, Charles Wesley. "One Cent Reward. Ran Away from the subscriber, on or about the 12th of April [1875], a colored boy names Charles Wesley Gage, an indentured apprentice. All persons are hereby cautioned not to harbor or trust the said boy. Charles Worthington." (Ref: *The Aegis & Intelligencer*, 30 Apr 1875)

One Cent Reward.

RAN AWAY from the subscriber, on or about the 12th of April, a colored boy named CHARLES WESLEY GAGE, an indentured apprentice. All persons are hereby cautioned not to harbor or trust the said boy.
ap16-3t CHARLES WORTHINGTON.

Green, Frank. "Five Cents Reward. Ran Away from the subscriber, on the 24th of September, 1877, a colored boy names Frank Green, eighteen years of age, indentured to Miss Sue Davis. All persons are hereby cautioned not to harbor or trust said boy. The above-named reward will be paid for his return. Thomas H. Roberts, M.D., Churchville P. O." (Ref: *The Aegis & Intelligencer*, 5 Oct 1877). [This may have been Franklin Green (b. 10 May 1860), son of Minty Green. (Ref: Harford Indentures Book WSB No. 1)]

FIVE CENTS REWARD.

RAN AWAY from the subscriber, on the 24th of September, 1877, a colored boy named Frank Green, eighteen years of age, indentured to Miss Sue Davis. All persons are hereby cautioned not to harbor or trust said boy. The above reward will be paid for his return.

THOMAS H. ROBERTS, M. D.,
oct5-3t Churchville P. O.

Hanson, Charles. 1878. "Ten Cents Reward. Ran Away from the subscriber, residing near Jarrettsville, a colored boy, name Charles Hanson, about 16 years of age, an indentured apprentice to John B. Ware. All persons are warned not to harbor or trust said boy on my account. – Ten Cents Reward will be paid for his return. John B. Ware." (Ref: *The Aegis & Intelligencer*, 28 Jun 1878)

Ten Cents Reward.

RAN AWAY from the subscriber, residing near Jarrettsville, a colored boy, named CHARLES HANSON, about 16 years of age, an indentured apprentice to John B. Ware. All persons are warned not to harbor or trust said boy on my account.—Ten Cents Reward will be paid for his return.

je14 3t* JOHN B. WARE.

Harris, Solomon. "$40 Reward! Will be paid for the arrest of two Negro Boys, apprenticed by the Orphans' Court of Harford County to learn the Farming business. – Solomon Harris is quite black, 5 feet 10 or 11 inches high, aged between 19 and 20 years; can speak some German, and is ruptured in the groin. Geo. W. Watkins is about 17 years old, tall for his age, 5 feet 8 or 9 inches high, talks thick, and is a delicate boy. – Both have blue blouses and drab pantaloons and Sol has a suit of black clothes. Forty Dollars Reward will be paid for the arrest and return of both, or $15 for Sol and $25 for George. All persons are forewarned from harboring these bots, as I will enforce the penalty of the law against such as far as I can. – If there are any necessary prison fees they will be paid. These boys left the subscriber on the 24th of January. John S. Dallam. Bel Air, Md., Jan. 30th, 1864." (Ref: *Southern Aegis*, 12 Feb 1864)

Hopkins, Gilbert Bradford. "One Cent Reward. Ran Away from the subscriber, on the 5th of January, 1869, a colored Boy named Gilbert Bradford Hopkins, an indentured Apprentice. The public are hereby warned not harbor said boy, under penalty of the law. Wm. M. Ady, near Mill Green." (Ref: *The Aegis & Intelligencer*, 29 Jan 1869)

ONE CENT REWARD.

RAN AWAY from the subscriber, on the 5th of January, 1869, a colored Boy named GILBERT BRADFORD HOPKINS, an indentured Apprentice. The public are hereby warned not harbor said boy, under penalty of the law.

WM. M. ADY,
Near Mill Green.

jan22 3t

Morgan, William Henry. "Six Cents Reward. Ran Away from the subscriber, on the night of Saturday, the 13th of June [1863], a bound Negro Boy named William Henry Morgan – nineteen years old, about 6 *(sic)* feet 9 inches in height [most likely 5 feet 9 inches tall], of very dark color, and had on when he left, dark clothes. All persons are hereby warned not to trust or harbor said boy. John V. St. Clair, Jarrettsville, Harford Co., Md." (Ref: *The Southern Aegis*, 26 Jun 1863)

SIX CENTS REWARD.

RAN AWAY from the subscriber, on the night of Saturday, the 13th of June, a bound NEGRO BOY named William Henry Morgan—nineteen years old, about 6 feet 9 inches in height, of very dark color, and had on when he left dark clothes. All persons are hereby warned not to trust or harbor said boy.

JOHN V. ST. CLAIR,
Jarrettsville, Harford Co., Md.

Mullen, Elizabeth. "Five Cents Reward. The public are warned not to harbor or trust on my account Elizabeth Mullen, colored, an Apprentice an indentured to the subscriber by the Orphans' Court of Harford County, who left on or about the 1st of August last [1876]. A reward of five cents will be paid for her return. John J. Gladden." (*The Aegis & Intelligencer*, 6 Oct 1876)

FIVE CENTS REWARD.

THE public are warned not to harbor or trust on my account ELIZABETH MULLEN, colored, an apprentice indentured to the subscriber by the Orphans' Court of Harford county, who left on or about the 1st of August last. A reward of five cents will be paid for her return.

sep22-3t JOHN J. GLADDEN.

Negro Joseph. "Runaway. Run away from the subscriber, on the 27th of August, 1872, a colored boy named Joseph, about 13 years old, bound to Alexander Y. Watters, deceased. All persons are warned not to harbor or credit said boy, on account of estate of deceased. James W. Wetters [actually Watters], C. E. Watters, administrators. (Ref: *The Aegis & Intelligencer*, 6 Sep 1872)

Runaway.

RUNAWAY from the subscriber, on the 27th of August, 1872, a colored boy named JOSEPH, about 13 years old, bound to Alexander Y. Watters, deceased. All persons are warned not to harbor or credit said boy, on account of estate of deceased.

JAMES A. WETTERS,
C. E. WATTERS,

sep6-3t Administrators.

Parks, William. "10 Cts. Reward. All persons are hereby forewarned from harboring or employing a colored boy, named Wm. Parks, who ran away from the subscriber, on or before the 7th of [the] 4th month, 1874, as the Law will be strictly enforced. Geo L. Scott." (Ref: *The Aegis & Intelligencer*, 17 Apr 1874)

10 Cts. Reward.

ALL persons are hereby forewarned from harboring or employing a colored boy, named WM. PARKS, who ran away from the subscriber, on or before the 7th of 4th month. 1874, as the Law will be strictly enforced. GEO. L. SCOTT.
ap17-4t

Selby, Robert. "Ran Away from the subscriber on Saturday Feb. 18th, 1882, a Colored Boy, named Robert Selby, about 14 years of age, and having nearly four years to serve. All persons are warned not to hire or harbor this boy. A reward of $1 will be paid for his return. I. G. Mathews, Blenheim [near Havre de Grace], March 8th, 1882." (Ref: *The Aegis & Intelligencer*, 10 Mar 1882)

Ran Away from the Subscriber, on Saturday, Feb. 18th, 1882, a Colored Boy, named Robert Selby, about 14 years of age, and having nearly four years to serve. All persons are warned not to hire or harbor this Boy. A reward of $1 will be paid for his return. I. G. Mathews. Blenheim, March 8th, 1882. m10-2t

Simms, Joseph. "Five Cents Reward. Ran away from the subscriber, on or about the 25th of July, 1874, a Colored

Boy, named Joseph Simms, an indentured apprentice. All persons are hereby warned not to harbor or trust said boy, under penalty of the law. Robert Magaw, Abingdon P.O., Harford Co., Md." (Ref: *The Aegis & Intelligencer*, 28 Aug 1874)

Five Cents Reward.

RAN away from the subscriber, on or about the 25th of July, 1874, a Colored Boy, named JOSEPH SIMMS, an indentured apprentice. All persons are hereby warned not to harbor or trust said boy, under penalty of the law.

ROBERT MAGAW,
Abingdon P. O., Harford Co., Md.
au21-3t*

Watkins, George W. "$40 Reward! Will be paid for the arrest of two Negro Boys, apprenticed by the Orphans' Court of Harford County to learn the Farming business. – Solomon Harris is quite black, 5 feet 10 or 11 inches high, aged between 19 and 20 years; can speak some German, and is ruptured in the groin. Geo. W. Watkins is about 17 years old, tall for his age, 5 feet 8 or 9 inches high, talks thick, and is a delicate boy. – Both have blue blouses and drab pantaloons and Sol has a suit of black clothes. Forty Dollars Reward will be paid for the arrest and return of both, or $15 for Sol and $25 for George. All persons are forewarned from harboring these bots, as I will enforce the penalty of the law against such as far as I can. – If there are any necessary prison fees they will be paid. These boys left the subscriber on the 24th of January. John S. Dallam. Bel Air, Md., Jan. 30th, 1864." (Ref: *The Southern Aegis*, 12 Feb 1864)

Williams, John. "Five Cents Reward. Ram Away from the subscriber, on or about the 1st of September, 1878, an indentured colored Apprentice, named John Williams, 19 years of age. The public are hereby warned not to harbor or trust the said boy on my account. The above reward will be paid and no thanks given for his return. T. B. Swartz, near Abingdon." (Ref: *The Aegis & Intelligencer*, 22 Nov 1878)

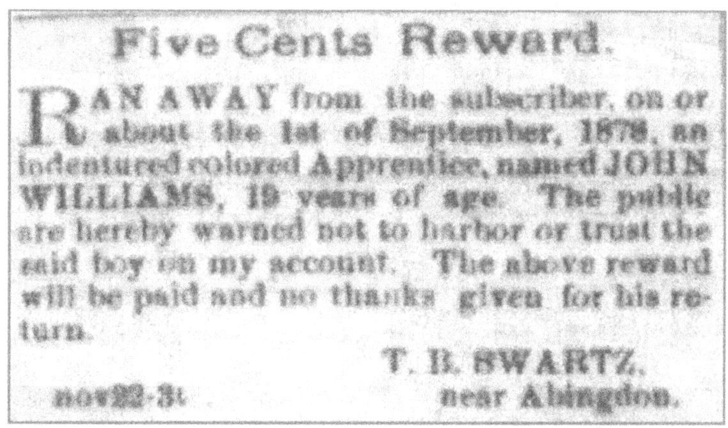

Five Cents Reward.

RAN AWAY from the subscriber, on or about the 1st of September, 1878, an indentured colored Apprentice, named JOHN WILLIAMS, 19 years of age. The public are hereby warned not to harbor or trust the said boy on my account. The above reward will be paid and no thanks given for his return.

T. B. SWARTZ,
near Abingdon.

nov22-3t

Known Harford County Accomplices in Slave Flight

Craner, David, was a slave accomplice circa 1858 [but he was not enumerated in the 1840, 1850, and 1860 Harford and Baltimore County Censuses]. (Ref: Maryland State Archives' On-line "Legacy of Slavery in Maryland")

Harris, "Had," was a free man and not a runaway slave, but he would help freedom seekers escape on the Underground Railroad. His house was located not far from Hopkins Creek at "Worthington's (Shure's) Landing [near

Darlington and Berkley in northeast Harford County] and was the 'jumping off place' for many a traveler on this railroad. As the fugitives made their way north … ["Had"] would row them up the Susquehanna River into Pennsylvania or across the Susquehanna where they would be met by other 'conductors' who led them to other 'stations.' The house was buried under the waters of Conowingo Lake when the dam was built in 1928. The image below was taken in 1890 and Jean Sharpless Ewing indicated it was the Richard "Had" Harris house. (Ref: *A Journey Through Berkley, Maryland*, by Constance R. Beims and Christine P. Tolbert, 2003, p. 44). Other sources, however, including local historian Samuel Mason, Jr.'s *Historical Sketches of Harford County, Maryland* and Maryland State Archives' on-line project *Legacy of Slavery in Maryland*, both state it was Hazzard "Had" Harris. Therefore, additional research will be necessary before drawing any further conclusions.

Mason, Samuel, Jr. (1887-1957), of Darlington, wrote the following in 1955: "Underground Railway. – Liberty is exemplified pure and simple in the unconfined maniac, unhampered by control or inhibitions and liberty as such all will agree to be of questionable value. On the other hand, if we load a man with chains, he is really no more a slave than the man loaded with inhibitions. When Lincoln gave the negro freedom during the Civil War, he did not by and large, free him from hard work or mental misery, but by placing his destiny in his own hands, he liberated be impossible. Fifty years previous to the Civil War the Society of Friends became aware of this state of affairs and urged its members to free their slaves, which they largely did, and members of their Society were therefore indefatigable in aiding the runaway slaves in their dash for freedom to Canada. This movement for freedom by the slaves was of slow growth, perhaps increasing system in the South. At all events more and more slaves slipped across the border each year and they were numbered by the thousands, but it was not until the passage of the Fugitive Slave Law in 1850 that the situation was brought forcibly to the attention of the Nation as a whole. Vigilance Committees were organized available for the fugitives, who were constantly passing North towards Canada. Routes were determined and Stations prepared along the way where Colored people could be cared for and aided. As a rule, the escaping slave had to depend on himself and the North Star until he reached the Pennsylvania or Ohio line and then singly or in batches of from fifteen or twenty, they were passed on in covered carriages or under straw in farm wagons. The fare from Baltimore to York, Pennsylvania was forty dollars as the risk was high, particularly after the passage of the Fugitive Slave Law. Thomas Garrett, a Friend living in Wilmington Delaware, was finally arrested and forced to pay a heavy fine for his abolitionist practices, although even this did not deter him from constant efforts along these lines. My own grandfather was twice arrested for helping slaves in Philadelphia, but nothing could be proved against him. [underlining added]. Many slaves crossed from Maryland into Gettysburg and York, which were the nearest stations to the border. Some of these slaves would be hidden by the Quakers and then passed on by night. So great was the exodus at Columbia that slave owners posted men along the route and paid teamsters to give information, but all to no avail. In our part of Harford County, one of the routes across the river was at Worthington's Landing. The road leading down to it may be seen today as it descends the river hill immediately below the Conowingo power house. William Worthington lived in the house recently owned by Edward S. Shure, since torn down, and in the evening frequently one of his men would come to him and whisper, "Uncle Billy there's people on the hill," thereupon Uncle Billy would order a sheep killed and cooked for the escaping slaves then hiding, in the cornfields, and after dark a boat would be available at the landing to take them across the river. A colored man by the name of Had Harris undertook this service. His house formerly stood beside the canal and the recent paper mill. The accounts of the escape of slaves, and I have hundreds of them, are essentially alike. They "Just got tired of it," One slave at least, escaped from the Hayes property at Shuck's Corner and several others left the farm of Dr. Abraham Street near the Rocks. Their mistresses were the worst offenders as a rule, and many of them showed little mercy." (Ref: *Historical Sketches of Harford County, Maryland*, by Samuel Mason, Jr., 1955, pp. 116-118)

Smith, Gideon G. (1808-1885). A Quaker, "Gideon Smith, of Swallowfield [located in Berkley] operated one of those [Underground Railroad] stations, strategically located near a heavily wooded area, about a mile from the Susquehanna River and ten miles from the Mason-Dixon Line. This location and the abolitionist temperament of the owners of Swallowfield were a natural fit for providing a safe haven on the Underground Railroad network. According to Elizabeth Sharpless Ewing, Gideon Smith's granddaughter, the phrase 'There are people in the corn' was the signal to prepare for the fugitives." [They hid in the ice house.] (Ref: *A Journey Through Berkley, Maryland*, by Constance R. Beims and Christine P. Tolbert, 2003, p. 42). [Gideon G. Smith is buried in nearby Darlington Cemetery.]

Swallowfield Ice House (by artist John Sauers)

Torrey, Charles T. "Charles T. Torrey was an abolitionist who conducted slaves to freedom through Harford County in 1842-1844. His usual route was Baltimore to Bel Air to Deer Creek and then Peach Bottom, where they crossed the river [into Pennsylvania]. He was ultimately arrested in June 1844 and sentenced to prison." (Ref: Letter dated 1 Sep 2009 from E. Fuller Torrey, M.D., of Bethesda, MD, to The Historical Society of Harford County in Bel Air, MD)

Worthington, William. "Worthington's Landing, located along the banks of the Susquehanna River on the Harford County side, was one of the routes up the Susquehanna River north to Pennsylvania. The Conowingo Power Plant [Dam] now occupies the land. Samuel Mason gave this account of 'Uncle Billy' [William Worthington]: 'In the evening one of his men would come to him and whisper, Uncle Billy, there's people on the hill; thereupon Uncle Billy would order a sheep killed and cooked for the escaping slaves then hiding in the cornfields, and after dark a boat would be available at the landing to take them across the river.'" (Ref: *A Journey Through Berkley, Maryland*, by Constance R. Beims and Christine P. Tolbert, 2003, p. 44)

Index to Other Names Within the Text

Heritage Books by Henry C. Peden, Jr.:

1890 Reconstructed Census of Harford County, Maryland, Volume 1: A-J

1890 Reconstructed Census of Harford County, Maryland, Volume 2: K-Z

A Closer Look at St. John's Parish Registers [Baltimore County, Md.], 1701–1801

A Collection of Maryland Church Records

African-American Freedom Seekers: Harford County, Maryland, 1774–1864

A Guide to Genealogical Research in Maryland: 5th Edition, Revised and Enlarged

Abstracts of Marriages and Deaths in Harford County, Md., Newspapers, 1837–1871

Abstracts of the Ledgers and Accounts of the Bush Store and Rock Run Store, 1759–1771

Abstracts of the Orphans Court Proceedings of Harford County, 1778–1800

Abstracts of Wills, Harford County, Maryland, 1800–1805

African American Cemeteries in Harford County, Maryland

Anne Arundel County, Maryland, Marriage References 1658–1800
Henry C. Peden, Jr. and Veronica Clarke Peden

Baltimore City [Maryland] Deaths and Burials, 1834–1840

Baltimore County, Maryland, Overseers of Roads, 1693–1793

Bastardy Cases in Baltimore County, Maryland, 1673–1783

Bastardy Cases in Harford County, Maryland, 1774–1844

More Bastardy Cases in Harford County, Maryland, 1773–1893

Bible and Family Records of Harford County, Maryland, Families: Volume V

Biographical Dictionary of Harford County, Maryland, 1774–1974:
Over 1,200 Sketches of Prominent Citizens during the First 200 years of the County's History with Seventeen Appendices Listing Public Officials from 1774 to 2020
Henry C. Peden, Jr. and William O. Carr

Cecil County, Maryland Marriage References, 1674–1824
Henry C. Peden, Jr. and Veronica Clarke Peden

Children of Harford County: Indentures and Guardianships, 1801–1830

Colonial Delaware Soldiers and Sailors, 1638–1776

Colonial Families of the Eastern Shore of Maryland
Volumes 5, 6, 7, 8, 9, 11, 12, 13, 14, 16, and 19
Henry C. Peden, Jr. and F. Edward Wright

Colonial Families of the Eastern Shore of Maryland: Volume 21 and Volume 23

Colonial Maryland Commissions, Appointments and Other Proceedings, 1726–1776

Colonial Maryland Soldiers and Sailors, 1634–1734

Colonial Tavern Keepers of Maryland and Delaware, 1634–1776

Dorchester County, Maryland, Marriage References, 1669–1800
Henry C. Peden, Jr. and Veronica Clarke Peden

Dr. John Archer's First Medical Ledger, 1767–1769, Annotated Abstracts

Early Anglican Records of Cecil County

Early Harford Countians, Individuals Living in
Harford County, Maryland. in Its Formative Years
Volume 1: A to K, Volume 2: L to Z, and Volume 3: Supplement

Family Cemeteries and Grave Sites in Harford County, Maryland, (Revised Edition)

Farm Directory, 1774–2024, Harford County, Maryland

First Presbyterian Church Records, Baltimore, Maryland, 1840–1879

Frederick County, Md., Marriage References and Family Relationships, 1748–1800
Henry C. Peden, Jr. and Veronica Clarke Peden

Genealogical Gleanings from Harford County, Md., Medical Records, 1772–1852
Winner of the Norris Harris Prize from MHS for the best genealogical reference book in 2016!

Harford County Taxpayers in 1870, 1872 and 1883

Harford County, Maryland Death Records, 1849–1899

Harford County, Maryland Deponents, 1775–1835

Harford County, Maryland Divorces and Separations, 1823–1923

Harford County, Maryland, Death Certificates, 1898–1918: An Annotated Index

Harford County, Maryland, Divorce Cases, 1827–1912: An Annotated Index

Harford County, Maryland, Inventories, 1774–1804

Harford County, Md., Marriage References and Family Relationships, 1774–1824
Henry C. Peden, Jr. and Veronica Clarke Peden

Harford County, Md., Marriage References and Family Relationships, 1825–1850

Harford County, Md., Marriage References and Family Relationships, 1851–1860
Henry C. Peden, Jr. and Veronica Clarke Peden

Harford County, Md., Marriage References and Family Relationships, 1861–1870
Henry C. Peden, Jr. and Veronica Clarke Peden

Harford County, Md., Marriage References and Family Relationships, 1871–1875

Harford County, Md., Marriage References and Family Relationships, 1876–1880

Harford County, Md., Marriage References and Family Relationships, 1881–1885

Harford County, Md., Marriage References and Family Relationships, 1886–1889

Harford (Maryland) Homicides: Cases of Murder and Attempted Murder:
Committed by Men and Women Who Were "Seduced by the Instigation of the Devil"
in Harford County, Maryland During the 18th and 19th Centuries

Harford (Maryland) Suicides: Cases of Self-killings and
Attempted Suicides Committed by Men and Women Who Suffered from an
"Aberration of the Mind" in Harford County, Maryland, 1817–1947

Harford (Old Brick Baptist) Church, Harford County, Maryland,
Records and Members (1742–1974),
Tombstones, Burials (1775–2009) and Family Relationships

Heirs and Legatees of Harford County, Maryland, 1774–1802

Heirs and Legatees of Harford County, Maryland, 1802–1846

Inhabitants of Baltimore County, Maryland, 1763–1774

Inhabitants of Cecil County, Maryland 1774–1800

Inhabitants of Cecil County, Maryland, 1649–1774

Inhabitants of Harford County, Maryland, 1791–1800

Inhabitants of Kent County, Maryland, 1637–1787

Insolvent Debtors in 19th Century Harford County, Maryland: A Legal and Genealogical Digest

Joseph A. Pennington & Co., Havre De Grace, Maryland, Funeral Home Records: Volume II, 1877–1882, 1893–1900

Kent County, Maryland Marriage References, 1642–1800
Henry C. Peden, Jr. and Veronica Clarke Peden

Marriages and Deaths from Baltimore Newspapers, 1817–1824

Maryland Bible Records, Volume 1: Baltimore and Harford Counties

Maryland Bible Records, Volume 2: Baltimore and Harford Counties

Maryland Bible Records, Volume 3: Carroll County

Maryland Bible Records, Volume 4: Eastern Shore

Maryland Bible Records, Volume 5: Harford, Baltimore and Carroll Counties

Maryland Bible Records, Volume 7: Baltimore, Harford and Frederick Counties

Maryland Deponents, 1634–1799

Maryland Deponents: Volume 3, 1634–1776

Maryland Prisoners Languishing in Goal, Volume 1: 1635–1765

Maryland Prisoners Languishing in Goal, Volume 2: 1766–1800

Maryland Public Service Records, 1775–1783: A Compendium of Men and Women of Maryland Who Rendered Aid in Support of the American Cause against Great Britain during the Revolutionary War

Marylanders and Delawareans in the French and Indian War, 1756–1763

Marylanders to Carolina: Migration of Marylanders to North Carolina and South Carolina prior to 1800

Marylanders to Kentucky, 1775–1825

Marylanders to Ohio and Indiana, Migration Prior to 1835

Marylanders to Tennessee

McComas Funeral Home Interments, 1901–1941, Harford County, Maryland

Methodist Records of Baltimore City, Maryland: Volume 1, 1799–1829

Methodist Records of Baltimore City, Maryland: Volume 2, 1830–1839

Methodist Records of Baltimore City, Maryland: Volume 3, 1840–1850 (East City Station)

Ministers Directory, 1774-1924, Harford County, Maryland

More Maryland Deponents, 1716–1799

More Marylanders to Carolina: Migration of Marylanders to North Carolina and South Carolina prior to 1800

More Marylanders to Kentucky, 1778–1828

More Marylanders to Ohio and Indiana: Migrations Prior to 1835

Orphans and Indentured Children of Baltimore County, Maryland, 1777–1797

Outpensioners of Harford County, Maryland, 1856–1896

Presbyterian Records of Baltimore City, Maryland, 1765–1840

Quaker Records of Baltimore and Harford Counties, Maryland, 1801–1825

Quaker Records of Northern Maryland, 1716–1800

Quaker Records of Southern Maryland, 1658–1800

Revolutionary Patriots of Anne Arundel County, Maryland, 1775–1783

Revolutionary Patriots of Baltimore Town and Baltimore County, 1775–1783

Revolutionary Patriots of Calvert and St. Mary's Counties, Maryland, 1775–1783

Revolutionary Patriots of Caroline County, Maryland, 1775–1783

Revolutionary Patriots of Cecil County, Maryland, 1775–1783

Revolutionary Patriots of Charles County, Maryland, 1775–1783

Revolutionary Patriots of Delaware, 1775–1783

Revolutionary Patriots of Dorchester County, Maryland, 1775–1783

Revolutionary Patriots of Frederick County, Maryland, 1775–1783

Revolutionary Patriots of Harford County, Maryland, 1775–1783

Revolutionary Patriots of Kent and Queen Anne's Counties, 1775–1783

Revolutionary Patriots of Lancaster County, Pennsylvania, 1775–1783

Revolutionary Patriots of Maryland, 1775–1783: A Supplement

Revolutionary Patriots of Maryland, 1775–1783: Second Supplement

Revolutionary Patriots of Montgomery County, Maryland, 1776–1783

Revolutionary Patriots of Prince George's County, Maryland, 1775–1783

Revolutionary Patriots of Talbot County, Maryland, 1775–1783

Revolutionary Patriots of Washington County, Maryland, 1776–1783

Revolutionary Patriots of Worcester and Somerset Counties, Maryland, 1775–1783

St. George's (Old Spesutia) Parish Harford County, Maryland Church and Cemetery Records, 1820–1920

St. John's and St. George's Parish Registers, 1696–1851

Slaves and Slave Owners, Harford County, Maryland, 1814: Information Gleaned from 1814 Property Tax Assessments and Supplemented with Data from Subsequent Manumissions, Slave Sales and Runaway Notices

Survey Field Book of David and William Clark in Harford County, Md., 1770–1812

Talbot County, Maryland Marriage References, 1662–1800
Henry C. Peden, Jr. and Veronica Clarke Peden

The Crenshaws of Kentucky, 1800–1995

The Delaware Militia in the War of 1812

Union Chapel United Methodist Church Cemetery Tombstone Inscriptions, Wilna, Harford County, Maryland

www.ingramcontent.com/pod-product-compliance
Lightning Source LLC
LaVergne TN
LVHW050642100826
845148LV00011B/1951

* 9 7 8 0 7 8 8 4 5 4 1 5 8 *